DO826662

PSYCHIC TAROT

About the Authors

For nearly twenty-five years, Nancy Antenucci (Between the Worlds, LLC) has been a tarot reader, teacher, and mentor for hundreds of clients and students. She was dubbed "one of the best psychics" of the Twin Cities by *Twin Cities Metro* magazine.

Melanie Howard is a psychic, a tarot reader, and a co-founder of the Hastings Blessings and Breathing Center, a teaching center for women that focuses on spiritual topics.

To Write to the Authors

If you wish to contact the authors or would like more information about this book, please write to the authors in care of Llewellyn Worldwide and we will forward your request. Both the authors and the publisher appreciate hearing from you and learning of your enjoyment of this book and how it has helped you. Llewellyn Worldwide cannot guarantee that every letter written to the authors can be answered, but all will be forwarded. Please write to:

Nancy Antenucci and Melanie Howard
c/o Llewellyn Worldwide
2143 Wooddale Drive
Woodbury, MN 55125-2989

Please enclose a self-addressed stamped envelope for reply,
or $1.00 to cover costs. If outside the U.S.A., enclose
an international postal reply coupon.

Many of Llewellyn's authors have websites with additional information and resources. For more information, please visit our website at:

www.llewellyn.com

PSYCHIC TAROT

Using Your Natural Psychic Abilities
to Read the Cards

NANCY ANTENUCCI
with MELANIE HOWARD

Llewellyn Publications
Woodbury, Minnesota

First Edition
First Printing, 2011

Cover design by Kevin R. Brown
Cover card art from the Mystic Dreamer Tarot by Heidi Darras
Cover eye image © iStockphoto.com/RTimages
Editing by Laura Graves
Interior illustrations by Llewellyn art department
Interior Tarot card images from the Universal Tarot by Roberto De
    Angelis, reprinted by permission from Lo Scarabeo

Llewellyn is a registered trademark of Llewellyn Worldwide Ltd.

Library of Congress Cataloging-in-Publication Data
Antenucci, Nancy, 1958–
  Psychic tarot : using your natural psychic abilities to read the cards
/ Nancy Antenucci with Melanie Howard. — 1st ed.
      p. cm.
  Includes bibliographical references (p.   ).
  ISBN 978-0-7387-1975-7
  1. Tarot. I. Howard, Melanie A. II. Title.
  BF1879.T2A56 2011
  133.3'2424—dc22
                                                    2010043003

Llewellyn Publications
A Division of Llewellyn Worldwide Ltd.
2143 Wooddale Drive
Woodbury, MN 55125-2989
www.llewellyn.com

Printed in the United States of America

This book is dedicated to Joe Hahn,
who showed me a loving path;
to Christopher, Alex, Evalyn, and Sam;
and to all loving Seers, born and unborn.
—NANCE

For my parents, Mary Kay Humbert and Patrick Howard,
who first taught me the journey of faith
is not always a straight path.
—MEL

There are two forms of Magic:
one in which you add water and stir,
the other in which you plant carefully, water, and let grow.
If you are willing to follow the second,
you will find this book most pleasing.

CONTENTS

Acknowledgments

We wish to thank Barbara Moore for asking us to do this book in the first place; Tim Breslin and Karen Erickson, our ruthless and loving reviewers; Taste of Thailand in St. Paul for keeping us supplied with curry and water with orange slices for hours; Amy Bisonette, literary lawyer extraordinaire; Alexander, Allen, Andrej, Carole, Christopher, Corrine, David, Ira, Jason-Aeric, Karen M., Karen Q., Lisa F., Mary Kay, Mick, Rita, Sharon, Steve, Susan, and Suzi for their insights and support; the Tarot tribe; and last but not least, the Sleeping Goddess and the Desert Goddess we found within each other.

BEFORE YOU BEGIN

*With your heart as your compass,
your journey begins…*

To properly experience this book, you will need a creative mind, an adventurous spirit, and an open heart. *Psychic Tarot* encourages just as much exploration of your own spirit and journey as it does of your tarot cards. Seekers of truth, welcome.

The seeds of this book were planted twenty-five years ago, when I picked up tarot and started a very long and fruitful journey of being a reader, teacher, and mentor. I have become a frontline reader: I'm the one who's helping a mother decide which school would be good for her child. I'm the one who helps somebody who would like to get involved in politics have the courage to do so. I'm the reader for the everyday person. I love the responsibility of supporting others in becoming their own Creative Authorities. My intent in writing this book is to give you the confidence and inspiration to find your own voice.

The need for this book became clear a couple years ago. I was at the Readers' Studio—an annual conference hosted by the Tarot School—during a breakfast roundtable hosted by Rachel Pollack. In her usual provocative manner, she asked us if we considered ourselves to be psychic. To my surprise, most readers answered, "No." It wasn't until that moment I could believe I'd have anything more to say about being psychic than anyone else would. It is very important all of us, professional reader or not, be more open to our unique psychic potential. The world needs this expression more than ever. If we can transform ourselves and break the patterns that hold us in fear, then perhaps the liberated creativity will change the world for the better.

Naming and claiming this creativity as "psychic" is the first step in nurturing mindful intuition. It's a specific radio channel. It is the Sight, because you are seeing differently. You are seeing the invisible. I think the Sight makes a lovely blend with tarot, which provides very strong imagery. It's a good balance between the visible and the invisible. For this reason, I will be using the terms "Sight" and "psychic" interchangeably.

Throughout the book, there are stories illustrating certain concepts and ideas. Most names in these stories have been changed, but each story is true.

Before going on, I would like to add that this book would not have been possible without the help of my sacred scribe, Melanie. After a year of mentoring her through my own style of reading, I felt confident I had much to share with other curious minds and open hearts like hers.

How to Use This Book

There are many wonderful beginner's books with definitions of each card. I heartily recommend these books when you are ready to study the tarot craft. I hope this book will encourage you to begin trusting your own Creative Authority. At this point, in order to develop that trust, I suggest that you don't yet study card definitions. Commit to a time of exploring your own perceptions with the cards and your Sight. It is highly recommended to start your own book of tarot by creating a tarot journal. Besides creating your own book of definitions, you will also capture the cards' first impressions, a valuable reference. Simply dedicate a huge spiral notebook to any notes, ideas, and exercises you find in this book. A few pages per card might serve as a useful section as well. Hopefully, *Psychic Tarot* will trigger many creative realizations that will aid in gaining self-confidence in your abilities as a loving, healing reader. You will develop a long-term friendship with your cards, and these early impressions will provide a good foundation for that relationship.

This process is not like the sun—bright light that adds growth and gives us sustenance. This book is much more like the moon—it only illuminates, softly showing figures, and is something you will sense rather than know. It really is about trusting what you sense. Track any ideas or images in your journal as well as exercises. The teacher within you will awaken.

You will also need a tarot deck of your own that inspires you. The various images and art styles need to spark your creativity. If you need to buy a deck, look through all the cards first. Each card should tell you a story. This is the first step in learning an intuitive language. I would recommend not learning your initial tarot journey with a deck whose suit cards show a number of objects rather than a pictorial scene. Your choice of deck will be unique and personal. For your convenience, the Universal Tarot by Roberto De Angelis is illustrated in Appendix A. This deck (one among the very many!) will be used throughout this book for consistency.

Using your Sight with the tarot is an amazing way to pour your life into its stories. Your reality counts, and how you perceive and experience life matters. Your experience is not something you have to put aside so you find the sacred or holy path. Your human reality *is* your holy path. Tarot is a powerful tool in teaching us how to be fully human.

In many ways, this book is about helping you create your own style. There will be ideas that resonate. Other ideas may take more time to absorb or won't be useful for you. Trust your own heart and common sense at all times.

Use this book at your own pace. If you read it and put it down for a while, trust that rhythm. Allow gestation. Don't be disappointed if every idea doesn't take off right away. This is not a book you read through once. You will need to return to some chapters over and over again. Just know you are planting seeds—they will come up when you are ready.

If you aren't a seasoned reader, we encourage you to reference the chapter on boundaries, chapter 19, before reading for others.

One last thought. Consider asking a companion or group to join you on this journey. That way, you can talk about your experiences, mull over ideas, and share your journal. Also, sometimes it really helps to process out loud.

Blessings on your journey. Let's begin.

—Nancy

1

BLOCKS

Letting go of old ideas and restrictions

I walked into a verdant wood beneath a full moon at night. Between the trees I could see a fire dance amidst a merry caravan of dark-haired gypsy men. Their clothes were strange and their hair was long, and they danced and sang and spoke in tongues I didn't understand. Among the dancers was a scarved, graying woman with gnarled fingers and hawkish eyes. I did not speak or make a sound, but she saw through the darkness regardless and beckoned me to join the band. The dancers melted from the clearing, and a cloth, brightly colored with strange symbols, was laid upon the ground. As the music faded into the breeze, the old woman bent and produced from within her skirts a magnificently carved wooden box. An ancient creak split the sudden silence as I knelt before her, and from the box she withdrew a tattered deck of cards.

"My family has practiced the tarot with this very deck," she said, her English barely understandable for her age and accent, "since before the Nile sprung forth in the desert. It was given to the mothers of my mothers by the Devil himself. It has been bathed in the blood of every hand that has held it, and the secrets it holds are older than time. With it, I will read your future, for I have seen greatness in you."

Her spotted, olive-skinned hands then shuffled the ancient cards and laid three out before me. "I see Death," she said solemnly, the nod of her head setting her hoop earrings to swinging. "The Tower, and the Ten of Swords. Death rides for you this night, and you will swiftly become his through a terrible betrayal."

She looked at me, her dark eyes searching out my soul.

"What say you?"

I studied the dancing scythe-wielding skeleton, the crumbling castle, and the bleeding back-stabbed man in the cards before me, then breathed a deep and solemn breath.

"I just have one question," I said. "Are you sure this deck didn't come from Barnes and Noble? 'Cuz I have one just like it at home."

———

Many misconceptions about tarot and psychic abilities exist. You will need to know how you feel about both before going deep into either. Jot down your current beliefs about psychic abilities and tarot cards. It will be helpful to know what you have been trained to believe and what you choose to believe. This self-knowledge becomes your Creative Authority—your unique expression of reality. Being connected to your own Creative Authority is paramount as a foundation for nurturing your own psychic abilities.

Everyone has Creative Authority, not only "chosen" individuals. One of the biggest myths about tarot and psychic ability is that you have to have a special calling for it. Some say you must have gypsy blood, you need to have inherited skills, or there is a right and a wrong way to sense information. These are all false assumptions. All humans are equipped with intuition to protect themselves. We all have perceived something we can't see, hear, or smell. Psychic ability is simply a honed intuitive skill.

How can everyone be psychic if only a handful of people call themselves psychic? Simple: Imagine a piano in every house. One can choose to play that piano, decorate it with a vase of flowers or framed photographs, or use it as a makeshift file cabinet! Those who choose to learn and practice music will use their piano well. The piano doesn't disappear if it's not used, it just gets dusty. Some people might feel called to use their psychic abilities just as some people feel drawn to play an instrument. The potential is within all of us.

It may surprise you to know that not all tarot readers consider themselves psychic. The cards incorporate many diverse systems such as astrology, numerology, and Jungian psychology, just to name a few. It is entirely possible to feel comfortable interpreting the cards using nonpsychic methods. There is no rule saying one must read the cards psychically.

Part of the problem is the term "psychic" itself is so misunderstood. It's become a code word to cover a lot of phobia-charged ideas. Does it mean you can sense thoughts? Does it mean you can see the future? See death? In that context, a lot of tarot readers are going to say, "No, I'm not psychic."

A pervasive fear that makes most people flinch at the word "psychic" is that a psychic can jump in your head and see what you're thinking at any time. While there may be some people who are very good at telepathy, the ability to read thoughts verbatim has little to do with what it means to be truly psychic. We transmit a lot more forms of energy than just our thoughts. A good psychic practitioner, much like a good therapist, adheres to a code of conduct. There is a need for respect and permission. With integrity, you should only use your gift for another person after receiving informed consent.

At the other end of the spectrum are those who do not fear psychics, but rather see them as a type of manipulator. They believe psychics read body language, profile people, or at worst, are good guessers. There are "psychics" out there who feed into this prejudice by doing exactly those things. But don't let them negate the fact that people with honest, true psychic abilities exist. Developing your own abilities is the polar opposite of manipulation. True psychics accept the flow and buzz of life energy; they do not attempt to twist it.

And life energy does flow. Another huge misconception about the Sight and tarot is that the future is set and predictable. "I'm going to see bad things." "I'm going to see my death." "I need to know if I'm going to be lucky." "I'm afraid to look at my future." These ideas come out of the false idea of a set future we are helpless to affect. Actually, we are all co-creating our futures. The true power of a reading is to help you see how you are creating your future right this minute. Where you are now and the choices you have are the results of decisions you've made before—it's all about choices.

Using tarot and the Sight is about making choices that facilitate healthy growth. When people don't want to see the "bad things," it's almost like they're saying, "I don't want to take ownership of some lousy choices I'm making right now." And sometimes people don't. Seeing the bad things can be almost as scary as seeing death, because that usually means a change is needed in your life. As for being afraid of death, there's no preparation for it except living well. The point of psychic tarot is not to predict death. It is to help you or a client to live life more fully.

In addition to discomfort over death and the Death card, tarot cards are generally misunderstood. A popular myth is the cards won't work unless they're given to you. It's a beautiful but quaint tradition that has probably kept many curious people at bay. The truth is, the cards will certainly work if you buy them yourself. They might even work better because you chose them yourself.

Another misleading notion is that each card has one very definite, fixed meaning. If this were true, it would be like saying a person has only one thing to say. Each card has a very specific essence with *many* things to say. Approach the cards as friends you don't know yet. As you might guess, they will never fail to surprise you with their mystery.

Just as there are no "good" people or "bad" people, there are no good or bad cards. The idea of good and bad cards is a very common prejudice. If you see the cards as good or bad, it will hinder your interpretations. Some cards might have a greater proportion of friendly energy, while others seem hard or edgy. However, keep in mind that there is always the potential for both in every card.

From hard-earned experience, I've found that you rarely change people's biases about using psychic and tarot gifts. Be in your truth and let them have theirs.

One of the most harmful myths about tarot and the Sight is that they conflict with the sacredness of religions. Whether you approach the cards as a hobby, as research into your own identity, or even as a spiritual practice, they never need replace your religious beliefs. Psychic tarot should only help you be a more loving and understanding person. When used well, it will. Opening your mind, heart, and soul to psychic energy does not mean flinging the doors wide open for evil to enter. You choose the rhythm and the pace. You are safe in love and can keep your boundaries. The darkest, scariest, most evil things are already within you—they are your fears. Facing them might be uncomfortable, but it is certainly necessary. You must have faith in your own strength and goodness, as well as courage, before undertaking this journey. You won't go far walking this path in fear.

2

❧

THE POWER OF A READING

In the moonlight, not everything is as it appears

The moon has a gravitational pull on the waters of our planet. A very similar dance happens between psychic energy and the imagery of the tarot. It is a dance of give-and-take, between what we sense and what we see in the cards. It can literally change lives, or at the very least, perspectives.

At the foundation of most readings is the question "What do you hope to change?" This isn't always something you'll know right away. Regardless of whether you're reading for yourself or someone else, this is a powerful question. Consider the idea that all energy comes from two sources—love and fear—and you can't operate from both at the same time. If you view the reading through this lens, choices become much clearer. The cards will reflect whether you move reactively through fear, or proactively through love. You gain a greater awareness of how you are living your life. This awareness offers choice.

Often I ask my client, "If I gave you a fully loaded magic wand, what would you change? What would you tap with this wand?"

~⚬∫⚬~

Reading for someone can feel like unrolling a beautiful map of choices. It shows choices they have made, are making, and could make. The past, present, and future all become the present, because all are being created in this moment. Stone Age ancestors demonstrated a similar concept of time when they painted bison on cave walls before they hunted them. As our early ancestors did, we can create choice by feeling, sensing, and honoring the essence of that which we desire. Through the cards, you can embrace and become your future self. This magic is as old as humankind. If you name it, you can claim it. Through a tarot reading, you help yourself and others to claim how they want to put their energy and focus into the world.

Reading the cards often helps people recognize old patterns of behavior, feelings, and thoughts. These habitual loops can be exposed through the fresh perspective of a reading. New creative thoughts allow new choices. On a larger scale, readings can suggest helpful new directions rather than being predictive. Affirmative insights encourage hope and love (and therefore empowerment) in every choice you make.

In this place where time is layered into one moment, be completely open. Don't censor any information you are given, even and especially if it doesn't make sense.

————

I did a reading for a woman named Donna who felt a little trepidation as a mother. She was sending her young daughter, Sage, off to New York, and wanted to know she would be all right.

We laid the cards down and looked at them. The pictures gave a very solid answer, but I could also tell that psychically, a bigger story was trying to come through. A phrase kept coming to me over and over: "Ripped heart. Ripped heart."

They were really graphic words, and I didn't want to use them. I assumed Sage would go to New York, fall in love, and have her heart broken. But instead of watering down what I heard, I followed my senses and stayed true to the words I had heard. The card that triggered the words was the Three of Swords. I told Donna that Sage would experience a ripped heart. I said it could very possibly mean Sage would fall in love and be very disappointed.

I offered a creative suggestion to do something soon thereafter. "Make it something really fun," I said, "so that Sage will have a reserve of good memories to fall back on when the time comes."

Donna followed my advice, also sensing something was needed. She took her daughter and some friends to Disney World and they had the trip of a lifetime. Her daughter went to New York shortly afterwards.

Unbeknownst to any of us, Sage had a rare heart defect. Her heart spontaneously, literally, ripped in half. She died on a sidewalk in New York.

Months later, Donna came back to me and told me this story. I was shocked. It was unbelievable that the words I'd heard were so specific and true. I was also in awe that due to that reading, Donna created one last wonderful memory with her daughter.

In that one moment, I vowed not to censor or reinterpret information received during a reading. I learned to trust messages that come from beyond and through the images from the cards. I'd become a believer in the transformative power of the psychic tarot craft.

3

✤

TAROT BASICS

Embracing your path

As an artist, you want to know something about your canvas. The tarot deck in your hand may be different from the one used in this book, but its origins are the same. Tarot began as a card game called *tarocchi*, which is still played in some parts of the world. The first tarocchi decks can be traced to fifteenth-century Italy. Records do not show tarot being used for divination until the sixteenth century.

The first tarot decks did not have a set number of cards. The suit cards were not illustrated. The "Trumps and the Fool" that we now call the major arcana did not have a fixed order. As a card game, tarocchi had set numerical values assigned to each of the cards. It was not until much later that someone (or several someones) assigned esoteric meanings to the cards. Those meanings have changed over time, and continue to evolve. Understanding this changing nature may free you to trust your own interpretations. One of the foundations of learning this way of reading is to slowly but surely trust your own authority. Creating your own foundation makes it easier to build on traditional meanings at a later time.

Most modern decks owe their beginnings to a little deck called the Rider-Waite-Smith (RWS), created by members of the Hermetic Order of the Golden Dawn in 1909. Arthur Waite wrote the definitions. Pamela Colman Smith, known as "Pixie," was the first to illustrate the suit cards. It may seem like a small change, but it revolutionized all of tarot. The deck was published by the Rider Company, and was henceforth known as the Rider-Waite, or Rider-Waite-Smith deck. The RWS was once the only deck available in the United States and is still widely used today. The deck you've chosen for this journey is likely a variation or descendent of the RWS.

As your deck is going to be your personalized tool, it's important to initiate it. The first step in caring for your deck is making a home for it. A traditional ritual is to find a wood box and to wrap the cards in silk, preferably black. Discard or store away the original box and place your cards in a pouch or special box, or wrap them in a scarf if you don't choose the traditional "home." Use a covering that means something to you and that you find beautiful. Occasionally, a deck may "tell" you what it wants to be kept in. Trust the voice and honor it.

If you received your deck from someone else, you may want to cleanse it or reenergize it like you would a battery. The idea is to make the deck yours and to imbue it with your energy. One way of doing this is to burn dried sage and let the cards be touched by the smoke. Another method to purify your cards is to leave them out on a ledge in the moonlight. You might even have your own tradition in mind. Any gesture you invent will make the deck ready to serve you.

Remember, these cards are *your* cards. You will need to determine who touches them, how, and when. For example, others should have your permission to look through them in your absence.

Another suggestion while you explore tarot is to read, study, and/or play with them when you are in a curious or hopeful state. There is a tendency to turn to the cards only when you are depressed, sad, or scared. It's better to approach them in many different states of mind. The cards are very much like good friends: you want to share the joy along with the pain.

While you're developing an intuitive style, it's going to be tempting to study tarot definitions through other books, on the Internet, or through the descriptions in the little white book that probably came with the deck. Try not to. The idea is to cultivate your own interpretations and to watch them flourish before seeding your tarot garden with other people's ideas. You have much to gain from your discomfort of not knowing. When you feel ready to integrate your understanding of each card with others' definitions, *Seventy-Eight Degrees of Wisdom* and *Tarot Wisdom* by Rachel Pollack are both excellent resources, as is Corrine Kenner's *Tarot for Writers*. They offer very thorough viewpoints on the symbolism and history of each card.

When choosing a tarot deck, there is a high probability you will be attracted to more than one. For the beginning of your journey, try to commit to one deck. As you progress, different decks will become much-needed artistic and philosophical assets. A professional reader will often have more than one deck for different needs, states of mind, or perspectives.

F OR MY CLIENTS, I OFTEN PRESENT SEVEN DECKS. I LIKE TO HAVE VARIETY, A MENU TO PICK FROM.

A great habit to develop from the very beginning is mindful intention while working with and exploring the cards. You will also want to find some kind of ritual that releases the energy of the experience. It can be as simple as drawing one last card or sitting quietly for a moment, then blowing out a candle or reshuffling the deck as you give thanks for the information gained. You will find a way that feels right for you.

Treat the cards as a tool that will increase in strength rather than as mere picture cards. Begin and end any session with respect and mindfulness.

4

THE MINOR ARCANA: THE FIRST FAMILY

*Our lives move in rhythms like the seasons,
eternal and changing cycles*

Tarot is a wonderful storybook composed of seventy-eight scenes. To help you learn about each card, it will be helpful to see them as three families: the major arcana, the court cards, and the minor arcana.

The major arcana are the cards labeled 0 through 21 with titles such as the Empress, the Magician, and the High Priestess. "Arcana" comes from the Latin *arcanum*, the word for "hidden" or "secret." The court cards are the "royalty" of each suit, often labeled Page, Knight, Queen, and King. These cards belong to the minor arcana, but have a very different purpose we'll explain later. Your deck may have a different way of labeling court cards. Other examples would be princess, prince, queen, and king; son, daughter, father, and mother; or something a little more "out there," such as server, teacher, healer, and master.

The minor arcana are the suit cards numbered Ace through 10 and are divided into four suits. Decks vary almost as much in naming the suit cards as they do in naming the court cards. For the purposes of this book, the suits will be called: swords, wands, cups, and pentacles. You may need to consult the literature of your deck to know its particular paradigm.

The Minor Arcana

Each suit symbolizes an element: air, fire, water, and earth. This is the very stuff that makes up life—the four foundations of the tarot system. As a profound reflection of life itself, these elements, in turn, relate to specific seasons and cardinal directions. You will ultimately determine these specific seasons and directions yourself, and can use this traditional layout in the meantime:

	Swords	Wands	Cups	Pentacles
Other Names	Spades Spears	Clubs Staves Rods Batons	Hearts Cauldrons Chalices	Diamonds Coins Stones Disks
Element	Air	Fire	Water	Earth
Attribute	Mind	Creativity	Emotion	Sensation
Season	Spring	Summer	Fall	Winter
Direction	East	South	West	North

The swords represent mental and communicative abilities, the element of air, and the direction of east. Picture a sword swinging through the air. The energy of our thoughts, our words, the way we communicate, and the way we think move much the same. An idea carries with it energy. When we speak, our words and ideas are carried on air. Swords also represent beginnings, since all change can begin with just one thought or awareness. Clarity is much like the dawn of a new day. And as in spring, conception of all that will grow begins with consciousness.

Wands represent creativity and the element of fire. Wands are associated with the south and summer. In all of these traits—passion, creativity, and summer—we lose sense of time as we connect to a greater source. Wands are magic wands, like the trees that give them life. Trees are the beings that keep the earth rooted and oxidized. Our creativity does the same for us. It keeps us grounded and nourishes those around us. Also, trees, the wood of wands, catch fire. Our creativity is like flame in how it can shine new light and illuminate new perspectives. It also fires our imaginations and makes us burn with passion.

The cups represent the element of water and the direction of west. They represent emotion, flow, and feeling. Embodying autumn, cups also have a beautiful timeliness and inner landscape. Our emotions are the nectar of life held by the cups. They fill us, inform us, and we thirst for them. Emotions are our inner reality and the language of the heart.

Pentacles represent the element of earth, the everyday magic of sensations, boundaries, and form. Their place is north and their season is winter. Of the four elements, the pentacles can be the most symbolically elusive. It may help to think of the five-pointed-star—the pentacle—as the body, the form for the soul. Other perspectives of the suit of pentacles are as shields, stones, coins, or crystals. All of these materials are made from earth. The pentacle's ancient symbolic origin represents protection and boundaries. In that context, coins or money as a symbol for the earth suit is quite appropriate. Our culture puts a lot of emphasis on money, and it is a necessary boundary. You are not safe in our society if you do not have money.

These four elements inform all of tarot. The scenes speak of the little mysteries of life, the everyday lessons of love. Never underestimate the power these cards have to give you insight into your life.

Let's explore the power of the minor arcana through a reading. For those of you who have not yet attempted a reading, just go with the flow of your impressions and triggers. Record your thoughts. The following exercise is part of the Essence spread, which is helpful in becoming acquainted with each of tarot's three families.

The Essence Spread (Part One)

Separate the suits, Ace through 10, into the four elements. Put all the swords together, all the wands, the cups, and the pentacles. Don't worry about the order, and don't include court cards. When you have them separated, place the swords to the east, the wands to the south, the cups to the west, and the pentacles to the north. Place all four groupings face down.

You should have four distinct piles in front of you, looking something like this:

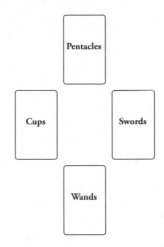

Take a few minutes to focus. Breathe and start to relax. Let go of the world and your responsibilities (they will patiently wait until you are done). Focus on relaxing your ribs, your belly, and your feet as you breathe. Try to switch off your "inner censor," which may feel like a little nagging voice that makes snap judgments, such as "this is bad" or "you have no idea what you are seeing or sensing." We will explore everything in much more depth, but for now, do your best to become a willing observer. Breathe and sink into yourself until you can quiet your mind.

Pick up the swords, still face down. Gently close your eyes. As you shuffle the swords, picture a beautiful blue sky in your mind. Any thoughts, responsibilities, or attachments you have will transform into a cloud, a bird, or the wind. Let them all float through this beautiful blue sky. As soon as the sky clears or you reach a place of neutrality, pick one of the cards and look at it. If it is upside down, turn it right-side up (reversed cards will be discussed later in the book).

Think of this card as a Kodak moment, showing how your mind is working and how you've been processing and/or expressing your thoughts and perceptions. Ask yourself:

Where are you in this card?

If you were to draw a picture resembling your state of mind and expression lately, would it resemble this card at all?

How does this picture or image describe your mental energy?

How do you sense the story of this card may parallel your reality?

What message/images are you getting from this card? Does the message ring true for you?

What did you secretly think or censor immediately?

Write down all your impressions in your journal.

Put the swords down, leaving the card you chose face up on its pile. Pick up the wands. As you shuffle them, think of the times you have felt most creative, most connected with your internal rhythms. Remember how you have experienced losing track of time in a delightful way. This might have happened during a creative act or a beautiful walk outside, or perhaps while listening to a song that speaks to your heart. Shuffle the wands until you feel very connected to your passion in life. Without looking, pick a card that has a similar charge about creative energy. Now look at it and ask yourself:

If you had to tell a story from this card—beginning, middle, and end—what would it be? Does it relate to your current life at all?

When you delve into the card's image, where are you being drawn?

Did you want a different image? If so, what would it have shown?

What does this card say about how you've been using your creative energy lately? Do you agree?

Again, write it all down.

Now let yourself go to the cups suit. As you shuffle, focus on your heart and breath. Really feel your heart as you visualize picking up a very holy cup. This cup will be full of the nectar you have been craving lately, the energy of an emotion that would nurture you. See yourself drinking from this cup and feeling satisfied, full, and regenerated.

When you're ready, keeping the cards face down, pick one card that feels most like the emotion that filled you. Look at the card, and ask yourself these questions:

Is this how you have been feeling lately? Is it something you haven't felt, or have been afraid to feel?

How does this reflect your emotional being?

Is there any similarity to the message you perceive from this card and the message your heart has been trying to get to you lately?

After writing, go to the pentacles. As you shuffle, see yourself standing firmly on earth, releasing all stress or fatigue. Feel grounded, nearly rooted. Sense. Ask your body what it would like to tell you. Slowly scan your body in your mind as you shuffle. Think about how it feels, and what your body has been doing for you lately. When you reach a point where your mind is quiet and you can be present, pick one card. As you look at that card, ask yourself:

What does this card say about your support or strength?

How is your current physical state depicted?

How much has your body been processing your emotional state? How does it feel about that?

What does this particular scene show you about how you've been using your body? What message is your body trying to give you?

Write down your impressions in your journal.

Now look at your cards and your answers as a whole. The minor arcana may have just shown you a pretty good picture of your present body/mind/spirit reality. It wouldn't hurt to jot down how the big picture looks to you. Congratulations, you've just done your first reading!

Light and Shadow Reading

Another exercise that offers excellent insight using only the minor arcana is the Light and Shadow reading. Pick two cards from each suit. One card represents where you are strong, highly developed, and natural. The other represents where you need more nourishment, awareness, or growth.

Again, rather than straining to remember specific meanings, just let the cards start to speak to you. The message does not need to be rational, it just needs to be true. These messages may speak very softly at first. Try to find yourself in the cards, as if you were the major protagonist in a tarot picture book. What parts do you relate to and really resonate with? Are there any aspects you strongly disagree with or that cause an emotional reaction? Know that you may heartily disagree with the cards you have chosen. Embrace the message for a day before dismissing it, however. It may have a perspective you need.

Every card has the potential to tell incredible stories about our lives, about the way we live. They are the episodes in our lives, the different energies and the different choices we make. The four elements are present in all aspects of our lives. As in learning any new language, thinking in that language becomes the shift needed to speak it fluently. To start thinking in tarot, start to see the world in four elements.

5

The Court Cards:
The Second Family

Seeing our humanity differently

The court cards are the second family of the tarot. Even though they belong to the bigger minor arcana, their position is completely unique. They represent humanity. This includes all the people in our lives, all relationships, as well as the many faces of ourselves. If tarot offers a blueprint to becoming a great person, then the court cards are all the actors and various roles we enact in the script of our destiny. Many would say these royal cards (or face cards) are the most challenging to read in a spread; after all, it's hard to be an impartial observer when dealing with other people.

Fear not, however. With some time and introspection, your court cards will serve as a vibrant palette of your understanding of humans and of human nature. These cards will also become mirrors to better understand yourself.

Traditionally, the court cards were the "significators" in a spread. A significator is a court card you would choose to either represent you or the client at the beginning of a reading. The significator would be the focal point that would inform the rest of the reading. Basic traits such as age, gender, hair color, or one's astrological sign were taken into account to choose the card best suited. This method is fun to use if you don't mind the restrictions. It isn't as popular these days, but this technique did provide a sturdy structure for each of the courts.

With newer decks come newer ways to interpret court cards, and newer images. Today's court cards vary widely in appearance, as well as in theme and title. Many decks refer to them as the page, knight, queen, and king. However, new labels are born every year with new decks. Some changes are small, such as swapping out the knight and page for prince and princess. Other decks have more radical changes. Here are a few examples:

Universal Deck	Page	Knight	Queen	King
Maat Tarot	Princess	Prince	Queen	King
Pagan Tarot	Elemental	Novice	Initiate	Elder
Tarot of Transformation	Server	Teacher	Healer	Master
Tarot of the Crone	Beast	Witch	Grand-mother	Shadow

The royal sixteen are strongly associated with their particular element. If each suit is a kingdom, then the court cards are the people of those kingdoms. The court cards and the elements together form a harmonious blend of humanity and the natural world, the hamlet carved out of the wild.

A Journey to the Courts

Take a moment to imagine the four elements. Sense each one by one. Open Air. Bright Fire. Soothing Water. Enduring Earth. Shift your focus into a bird's-eye view to watch each element grow so gigantic it becomes its own world, independent, pure, and primal. At the heartbeat of these elemental worlds will be a gathering of a human culture. Each of the four personalities represents and rules its society. Their essence has been captured, as if their photos were taken, to be the court cards of your deck.

Let's begin to explore these royal elemental beings from three perspectives. Like the other cards in the deck, you want to start seeing the definitions of your courts in layers. The first and most basic layer is to see the court cards literally as people and relationships in our lives. A second layer is one of archetypes that portray larger universal themes in ourselves and others. Finally, the courts can be interpreted as different kinds of energy. Your understanding and experience of others gives the court cards life and breath.

To aid in exploring who the court cards are in your world, you might consider creating columns or dedicating a specific page to each court card in your journal. Think of each court card as a blank canvas that needs the broad strokes from your own wisdom about yourself and others. Put time into acquainting yourself with each of them. And don't get too caught up in their physical appearance. As humans, we sometimes tend to see people as their color, gender, or age. Spirit is one of the last things we read on a conscious level. Start to sense the essence first. This way of acknowledging our fellow beings can open many new doors of insight. Spread out your court cards in front of you by grouping them by element as well as position. Your layout will look something like this:

1) People

Look at your court cards. Do you see any familiar faces staring back at you? Who would you choose to be your mother? Your father? Your sister? Your best friend? You might find a lot of them live in the same kingdom. This is natural. We seem to have certain preferences in the folks we gather near us. Jot down immediate impressions in your journal.

THE KING OF WANDS REMINDS ME OF MY DAD. HE IS A QUIET AND HUMBLE MAN WHO IS MOST COMFORTABLE IN NATURE.

Now go a little further. Write the names of all the people you can think of who have shaped you to be the person you are at this very moment. Assign each one a court card. Remember to stay connected to the essence, not the costume. For example, your favorite teacher may have been an older woman. You would perhaps select the Queen of Pentacles by looks alone, but her spirit is young, gentle, and lovely. If she feels like the Page of Cups instead, go with that impulse. There is no right or wrong selection. The whole system of the court cards is an organic reflection of your cast of characters.

Each of these sixteen cards is also an aspect of you! Jot down how each of these cards reflect you in some way. Which card do you most relate to as yourself? Which one is the ideal you? Which one is your private self? Who do you tend to feel like at work? Some courts may cause you to draw a blank for now, but will become clear in time.

I N MY REALITY, THE KNIGHT OF SWORDS
REPRESENTS MYSELF WHEN I'M BEHAVING
AS A WORKAHOLIC.

2) The Archetypes

Now consider the second layer of our royal ones. They present the archetypal energy of our everyday life. One can hardly describe the concept of archetypes without mentioning Carl Jung. He was a Swiss psychologist and psychiatrist and founder of Jungian psychology. Archetypes are innate ideas or patterns of the human psyche related to its development. Jung believed these psychic structures are wholly unconscious. One can examine these myths and stories that shape our psychological lives through art, imagery, religion, etc. In this way, the court cards are a most perfect form in capturing these different human essences.

If you were writing a script of your life and were not allowed to use any personal names, the archetypes would be the roles that you would assign to the various actors of your life. For example, rather than "William," you would go bigger to use the role he played, perhaps "the Lover." This archetypal way of naming experiences could also relate to the various roles you play in your own life, such as Daughter, Seeker, or Friend.

All these associations hold the wisdom you have gained in your own self-awareness and through being in relationships with others. Your ability to make these connections is essential because this knowledge extends through readings for others. For example, if the Queen of Cups represents your mother, she will now represent "the Mother." So when you read the Queen of Cups for others, it is possible you are reading about their mothers. The Queen of Cups has taken on a life as "mother" from your own life.

Scan the different chapters of your life. Imagine yourself as the script writer for a few minutes. Who were the leading actors? What was your role as the protagonist? What is the current chapter like? Some of the roles or archetypes could include:

The Shadow	The Vampire
The Worker	The Seeker
The Thief	The Anxious One
The Friend	The Wise One
The Sister	The Poet
The Brother	The Addict
The Teacher	The Golden One
The Trickster	The Healer
The Control Freak	The Mistress
The Boss	The Assassin
The Goddess	The Victim
The Warrior	The Censor

Jot down roles you have experienced either from others or within yourself, especially any that seem to repeat over and over again. Match each role with a specific court card.

WHENEVER I PULL THE QUEEN OF
PENTACLES, I RECOGNIZE HER AS
"THE THERAPIST." OFTEN SHE WILL
COME UP IN A READING TO SUGGEST THAT
THE CLIENT WOULD BENEFIT GREATLY FROM
TRADITIONAL THERAPY.

Positions of power can also be considered archetypal, such as that of leader, warrior, queen, and student.

The page learns from the knight. He isn't given much responsibility other than to take care of the knight, his horse, and weapons. When a page card turns up in a reading, this could mean the need to learn or study.

The knight is given orders as to where and when he will fight. He is not to question authority. He is a warrior, and his main focus is battle. His position is action. If during a reading you received a knight card as a response to what steps are needed, the message is speaking to some sort of necessary action. The message may literally be the "marching orders."

The queen knows the heart of the people. She gathers information by vision and listening to the needs of others. If the queen in a spread does not feel like she is a person or a facet of yourself, the cards may be displaying the need for vision and a response from the heart.

And we cannot forget the king, who has the final say, but also the ultimate responsibility for his kingdom. Often in a reading, a king represents the decision or commitment necessary for a productive strategy.

Compare the pages, knights, queens, and kings of the different suits to each other. What are the different ways of study and training amongst the pages? What kinds of protection and strength are demonstrated with the knights? How would you describe the vision of each queen? How does each king channel authority?

MY BEST FRIEND DENNIS WAS THE KNIGHT OF CUPS UNTIL THE DAY IT BECAME EVIDENT TO ME THAT HE HAD GROWN INTO THE KING OF CUPS.

3) Energy

A third option in interpreting the court cards (and every tarot card, for that matter) is to see them as pure energy. Each court could relate directly to you through its movement, gesture, color, etc. The way a knight rides his horse could trigger more associations than the knight himself. If you are drawn to what a person in a card is doing, it's quite possible it'll be the definition you will need.

As you look at each of the court cards, assign each one a verb. What is the action or mood of the card? Study the figures' body language, faces, gestures, colors, and their particular settings to receive clues about the cards' primal energies. For instance, do you detect a serene contemplation of one and the impulsiveness of another? Imagine you yourself are the court person. What would it feel like to be at a full gallop on a horse or to be sitting on a mystical throne by the ocean? It would be fun to mimic the court person's body positions. To try it, close your eyes and register how you feel or think.

Gender and age also connote certain kinds of energy. Don't be fooled by anyone's outward appearance. If you look at the court cards with unbiased eyes, you might be surprised to discover who is truly old and young, feminine and masculine.

Whether you view a court card as someone else, yourself, or primal energy, pay attention to any clues from your body. A very helpful question when you see a court card is, "Is this me, or is this someone or something other than me?" If you instantly relate to a card, have a physical reaction such as jumping, or resonate with it on a psychic or emotional level, the card is most likely a mirror for you. If it is somebody else, there is a sense of observing it from a distance. You won't feel it as much. Let us continue with the Essence spread to play with this concept.

The Essence Spread (Part Two)

Hold only your court cards as you close your eyes. Think of yourself falling like a feather, side to side as you drift to wherever your center is at this moment. Take all your energies in, and breathe.

As you shuffle the court cards face down, gently create a movie screen in your mind. Give yourself permission to view your life from a different angle. If you could be the ultimate observer of your life lately, what would that movie look like?

Ask for the images of people who presently have an effect on your life. It doesn't matter if they are alive or not. See the different scenarios appear on the screen. Observe your feelings and thoughts as you register each one. Gently avoid censoring or cleaning up any uncomfortable feelings.

Shuffle until your focus lands on one person or until you feel a special charge of one court card in particular. Look at the card. If you had someone in mind, does this feel like a match of some sort? Do you know who this might be? Is it you? What are you learning from your relationship with this person or this particular aspect within yourself right now? How is this card/relationship a good mirror for you?

The more you experience the richness of different relationships, the more open you become to understanding human nature within others and within yourself. Start to reverse the way you see humans by reading spirit or essence first. The next time you are standing in a checkout line, look at the row of folks next to you. Mentally assign each one a court card. Start with the basics. Ask which element they would be. Do they seem earthy or airy? Are they fluid or bright like fire? Which of the four positions would they hold? Would you give them the job of a student, warrior, visionary, or leader? In this way, you will start thinking in the tarot language, much like you begin thinking in a foreign language before you begin speaking it fluently.

6

THE MAJOR ARCANA: THE THIRD FAMILY

We are spirits seeking a human experience

The major arcana, or "greater secrets," are easily identified in any tarot deck. They are numbered 0 through 21 with very descriptive titles. These cards symbolize various forces of nature, great spiritual lessons, and different faces of the Divine. As we are both human and spiritual beings, we encounter these greater mysteries as guiding forces for our lives.

Of all the tarot families, this one most requires your Creative Authority. Definitions will ultimately need to come from you. Each one of these cards challenges you to embrace the mystery beyond this life so you can embrace the mystery in this life.

The major arcana are the "greater secrets" your heart and mind will experience somewhere along the way. In this way, we are very much like the Fool, the card at the beginning of this family. In some tarot philosophies, the Fool travels through each of the major arcana, learning and growing and living more in love. You might see yourself as the Fool attempting to read stories in the cards and listening to your heart's wisdom. You are made wiser in the attempt alone!

The following exercises may help you to better understand your major arcana. Have your journal ready. You won't want to miss any "aha!" moments.

Good Cop, Bad Cop

Take the major arcana from your deck and carefully examine each one. You will be drawn to certain cards. Separate all the cards that resonate strongly with you into one pile.

Some of the major arcana may alarm or distress you. If you are frightened, disgusted, or feel a different visceral rejection of any of the cards, separate those cards out into a second pile.

The last group will likely be the leftovers. If you don't have a strong feeling about a card either way, or you'd call its charge "neutral," or you find it just plain confusing, the card belongs in this third pile.

If you think of humans as spirits embracing the experience of living, the major arcana would be the forces of nature that help us all find that balance between human and spirit. Personified, these forces act as our teachers and guides. Out of each group, you will eventually choose one card. This card will represent a very specific teacher, teaching, or reflection of your life currently.

Hold your group of favorites. Find a focus within you as you look through this group to find the card that speaks directly to you. See in the reflection of this card any lesson(s) you are learning in your life right now that flow smoothly or offer little resistance. They might even be pleasurable. Go deeper into the card. What about it captured your eye? Your mind? Your heart? If this teacher were speaking to you, what would she or he sound like? What would you be taught? Imagine the teacher's energy was all around you, tutoring your spirit. What are you learning?

Now focus on the disliked group. Pick the card you consider the most offensive to your sensibilities. This card reflects the hard lesson(s) you are learning in your life right now. Rather than turn away from this card, try to examine it. If this is your challenging teacher, what is he or she demanding of you? Really pick the card apart. What bothers you about it? Is it the main character? Some outlying symbols? What is this card's difficult lesson?

Go to the neutral group. If you had to meet one, who would you choose? Look at that card, and imagine there was something in the air, but you couldn't quite define it. If there was a lesson or an energy that was shaping you, but you really just couldn't put a finger on the pulse, this card captures that ambiguity.

In tarot, you will be greatly served using the paradigm of "easy versus difficult" rather than positive/negative or good/bad. The goal of seeing with clear sight and moving through your life guided by your heart is to be at the place where you stand right now, truly and fully. Love teaches us in all the moments of our lives. There is not one place on the journey any more valuable than another. To be truly aware of your present state allows choices and growth.

With that in mind, look at your "easy" teacher. What would be a drawback to this teacher? A pitfall? What does she or he give or teach you that may not be helpful? Keep in mind that the easy lessons of our lives are not necessarily the most meaningful or important.

Now look at the "difficult" teacher. What is the true gift this teacher offers? Is it lasting? What is it that your personality or your temperament needs, and are you getting it from this particular lesson or teacher?

Next, look at the card of ambiguity. What if this card was completely clear to you and you understood its meanings? What would it say to you? What would you learn?

Read as deeply into these cards as you can, and record any new insights.

Play around with the concept of "easy" and "difficult." Start using them in your vocabulary more often. Quarantine the words "positive" and "negative" and "good" and "bad" for a while. The shift in focus will get you out of black-and-white thinking, and grant you new awareness.

The major arcana represent every moment that fundamentally changed you to become the person you are at this time. You may or may not experience all of these mysteries in this lifetime. For now, there is another exercise you can try to better acquaint yourself with the mysteries you may have experienced already.

Turning Point Exercise 1

Write down fifteen moments or events you consider the turning points in your life. These would be events or decisions that shaped you and made you who you are today. It could be as practical as going to college, or as esoteric as a dream that motivated you to make different decisions with your life.

When you have your list, spread out all of your major arcana face up. Absorb the symbols and colors. Get a feel for each card. Let your body go soft. Do you get a sense of which of these teachers/forces were with you at your different turning points? Which ones hold these experiences?

Now, sharpen your focus once more. Do you remember which cards stood out? Looking at your list now, can you find a card you feel represents each of the fifteen? There isn't a right or wrong answer. One card can repeat for different events. In fact, if you lay all the chosen cards out chronologically, you may even be able to detect a pattern. What cycle or lesson might you learn next?

Some people see these cards as faces of the Divine or as sacred energies. When you develop more personal connections to the major arcana, you will decide for yourself what they feel like to you.

Another way of learning the major arcana is to walk the journey. There are many versions of the path, some circular, some three-tiered, but most begin with the Fool (0) and end with the World (21). The Fool is often apart from the rest as though he were a traveler stopping at twenty-one different points.

The Fool's Journey exercise below may help you familiarize yourself with some of the more traditional views of the major arcana, but it can also give you a chance to create a more personal, unique connection to each of your cards.

The Fool's Journey

You are the Fool, asleep near the edge of a precipice.

At the dawn of a new day, something warm and wet tickles your nose. You reach up to rub it away, only to find a small, happy dog lapping your face. With a carefree laugh, you get to your feet, sling your pack over your shoulder, and start down the road. Your friend stays close at your heels.

Staring ahead, you wonder to yourself:

I wish I was heading towards…

A ways down the road, you come upon the Magician. He stands before an altar, commanding great energy and doing strange and wonderful things with it. Curious, you approach the altar. The Magician motions for you to hand over your pack. You do, and to your surprise, the Magician pulls four elements from your pack: earth, air, fire, and water. He transforms them with a fiery lightning bolt into a pentacle, a sword, a wand, and a cup. Over time, the Magician teaches you to master these elements and to use them in harmony.

When finished, the Magician returns the pentacle, the sword, the wand, and the cup. You stow them in your pack. The Magician asks you one last thing before you depart:

What are you becoming?

You find the path once more. It isn't long before the salty smell of the ocean, the call of seagulls, and the roar of waves smashing against the shore draw you to a seaside temple. You pass between two pillars—one white, one black—as you enter the temple. Seated within is the High Priestess. She bids you to approach. As you kneel before her, she holds out a scroll. The pomegranate curtain behind her ruffles in the sea breeze as you take the scroll, revealing a glimpse of a vast moonlit sea. For just a moment, you think the sea is not a sea of water but of scrolls just like this one. All the knowledge in the world might be contained in that sea.

You turn to the scroll and upon unrolling it, you realize it is your life's scroll. A message reveals itself as the High Priestess asks:

What do you secretly know?

When you are finished reading, she takes your scroll back and tucks it safely in her sleeve. Knowing you can return here whenever you need more insight, you take your leave of the High Priestess and continue down the path.

Birdsong and butterflies dance around you almost as soon as you have left the sea. Your dog chases a rabbit into the underbrush. As you bound after him, you come upon a very pregnant woman in rich robes, taking a turn about a wild, natural garden. The Empress takes a seat before you, and the rabbit scurries under her skirt. The dog stops and curls up at her feet, as though the Empress were his own mother. Lion and lamb lay down before her, and deer bound carefree through her garden. All are nurtured, loved, and cherished.

Neither of you speak at all, but simply enjoy the pleasant abundance of the garden. When you have fully absorbed its vibrancy, the Empress turns to you and asks sweetly:

What do you desire?

She waits for your answer, then directs you to the palace, the topmost tower of which you can see just above the trees. You are sad to leave the garden, but your spirits lift somewhat when the little dog resumes following you.

A pair of guards greet you at the doors of the great palace. One escorts you to the throne room, where you see an elderly but healthy-looking man sitting on the dais, his brow furrowed in thought. The crown seems large and weighty upon his head. A nearby table overflows with regimented stacks of papers, treaties, maps, and scrolls.  The Emperor gestures to a chair, and you sit before him. He tells you the story of his long reign, the difficult decisions he has faced, and the hard-won years of peace he negotiated. His wars were few, though there was no shortage of conflict during his reign. Fascinated, you hope even a tenth of his wisdom may rub off on you.

After his story is concluded, the Emperor sits back and looks deeply into your eyes. Before dismissing you, he asks a question:

What are you thinking clearly about?

The guards escort you back to the road. It isn't long before you hear a strange mix of sound. You follow the sound around a bend in the road to find a wide courtyard full of people in many different colorful robes. The religious of a thousand nations stretch in a wide arc along the edge of the courtyard. To your left, you see a man with a thick beard kneeling on a carpet and praying to Allah. Near him is a cardinal fingering his rosary and murmuring a prayer to the Lord. Beyond him is a Buddhist monk trickling colored sand onto a large earth mandala. Occasionally, one of the religious will come to the center of the courtyard and share teachings with the others. A whirling dervish soon comes to the center, his many-colored

robe flying up around him as he spins. The Sufi master stops before you. He extends his arms wide, encouraging you to take in the vast number of beliefs presented in this place. Then he asks:

What do you believe in?

You leave the courtyard, murmuring some of the prayers you have learned, and continue down the path. Soon you see another traveler resting beneath a tree. The little dog becomes excited and races over to the person. You chase your dog over to the tree only to find he is excitedly greeting the traveler. The traveler smiles. You

smile back. Together, you sit beneath the tree for hours, discussing life, and each other. Together you become the Lovers and decide to share your path for a while.

Gazing at your partner, the little dog, and the warm, wondrous day, you think to yourself:

I am in love with…

A bit further down the path, you come upon the Chariot. Or rather, it comes upon you. A cloud of dust heralds its arrival, and as you stand coughing, your eyes streaming, you see the charioteer race past. Two horses gallop ahead, always forward, their eyes reflecting the same determination of their driver. The charioteer commands both the animals, and though they seem a mismatched pair, he makes them move as one. The charioteer casts a glance over his shoulder as he speeds away. His words carry over the creak and rumble of the wheels.

What drives you?

When the dust begins to settle, you rub your eyes, and see another figure just ahead. Hefting your pack, you wander over to a beautiful woman. She seems calm, serene, and approachable. The dust settles, and you see she is not alone. You freeze in terror, seeing a lion at her feet. The creature is wild, and the look in its eyes tells you it could be vicious. You cry out, concerned for her safety.

She merely smiles and holds the lion's muzzle in her hands. The animal does not fight her. Flabbergasted, you ask this confident woman how this is accomplished.

She looks at you with wide, compassionate eyes. Instead of answering your question, she meets your gaze and asks:

What is your biggest challenge these days?

The woman and the lion wander away, leaving the path clear. The dog, which was huddled behind your leg, peeks his head out and gives a brave yip, now that the lion has gone. You scratch his head, and move forward. As you walk, the sun begins to set. The road becomes more twisted and tangled as it takes a turn through the woods. Soon, full dark is upon you, and not even a star can cut through the thick canopy of leaves above your head. You stumble, and lose the path. Surrounded by trees and unfamiliar scavenging sounds, you fear wolves. Uncertainty drives you to the edge of despair. Just when you are certain there is no hope, a light flickers through the trees.

You stagger toward the light, tripping over rocks and twigs and scraping your arms on tree bark. Soon the light becomes a lantern held in the hand of the Hermit. He holds out his hand to you, and you take it, expressing your gratitude for his light. The Hermit shakes his head, and tells you it is your light—you have known the way all along. He presses the lantern into your hands, and asks:

What does your inner voice tell you?

With the help of the lantern, you find the path once more. You follow it until you find a cave, and decide to rest for the night. As you enter it, the lantern light reflects a large, primitive painting on the wall. It is a large Wheel of Fortune, rife with strange characters and symbols. The Wheel appears to turn, showing the progression of  the seasons, the dawn and dusk of the day, and a person's birth and death. You trace the pattern of one figure on the Wheel of Fortune from humble beginning to rising success to crushing defeat and ultimate demise. It makes you wonder about your place on the Wheel.

Lately, I describe the circumstances of my life as…

In the morning, you leave feeling restored. Before long, you come upon the Hall of Justice. Justice herself sits before the hallowed halls of Law holding the Sword of Truth in her right hand and the Scales of Balance in her left. Her very presence is an overwhelming call for absolute honesty. You kneel at her feet, and say:

My greatest truth is…

Feeling lighter, you leave Justice and follow the path to where it curves into another wood. At the edge of the wood is a majestic old tree. A man has af-fixed himself to a branch upside down by his ankle. When you approach, you see the man is no mere mortal. You wonder if this may be some god meditating from the Tree of Life. You stand under the tree, and the man smiles at you. He invites you to join him.

Uncertain, but willing to try, you climb up and tie your own ankle to the tree. As you hang suspended, your perspective on the world changes.

As though sensing your revelation, your companion asks:

How do you see your life differently since ... ?

Armed with new perspectives, you climb down from the tree and enter the forest. The path leads you to a clearing, where you stop, shocked by the scene before you. Bodies litter the clearing, old and young, rich and poor. Riding among them is a skeletal knight on a white horse. When he turns and looks at you, you know instantly this is Death. And he is riding toward you.

Rooted to the spot, all you can do is stare as Death approaches. He reins his horse just before he would have mowed you down like the others in the clearing. Terrified, you can't force yourself to look at him, and look beyond him instead. Among the dead, you see white roses have begun to bloom. Heartened by this transformation from death to life, you look up at the skeletal rider. Death acknowledges your courage with a slight nod of his head. He asks:

What will you let die?

Then Death rides away, leaving behind him a field of white roses.

You cross the field and enter the trees once more. You find the angel Temperance standing directly in your path. A sense of grace overpowers you. As you watch, Temperance mixes water from two chalices. Impossibly, the water flows evenly back and forth between them. You wonder if you could temper some areas of your life in the same way.

The path beyond Temperance stretches into the distance, then disappears over a hill. You follow it with your eyes, imagining what might be in store. Temperance asks:

To what are you being guided?

Eager to find out, you leave the angel and race for the hill. You forget to pay attention to the path before you. Suddenly, the ground opens up and you feel yourself falling. You hit the ground with such force that you feel the ache in every inch of your being. When you look up, the blazing eyes of the Devil stare you down. In his hand, he holds your pack and your frightened dog. He seems to have the same hold on your life.

All around, people are chained to the Devil's throne. All manner of greed, addiction, and fear are woven into the chains. Even while the Devil laughs at you—his new puppet—you realize something strange: every collar binding each person to the Devil's throne is capable of slipping off if he or she has enough focus and courage. It slowly dawns on you that the Devil does not hold these people chained, but that each person has allowed their own fear and vice to enslave them.

Gathering your courage, you ask yourself:

What is my greatest fear?

You put your hands to the heavy iron collar around your own throat, and wrench it over your head, casting your fears aside.

The Devil bellows with rage, releasing both pack and dog. He is forced to let you go.

Shaking, you climb out of Hell carrying your pack, the dog following behind closely. It has taken you until nightfall to escape. The Tower stands before you, and you lean against it, gathering your scattered wits. You are out of the Devil's clutches, but you know in your heart that if you fail to change your approach or attitude towards some areas of your life, you will be right back at his feet. The Tower was built to sustain you, but now stands in the way of your thriving. You look up at it, standing right in the middle of your path, blocking your way. You say to yourself:

I seriously need to change …

Lightning strikes the Tower, and you jump back, watching it become reduced to a flaming pile of rubble. As you look at the ashes of the structure that took your entire life to build, you feel broken.

Just beyond the destroyed Tower, you see a glassy lake. You walk toward it, feeling sparks of hope. The Star shines brightly over the lake, where a beautiful nude woman pours water into the lake and onto the shore. She looks up at you and encourages you to embrace this short life.

I accept …

The woman vanishes in the light of the Moon as it rises over the lake, revealing as much as it conceals. Strange images form beneath the water's surface, distorted by moonlight and ripples. You see shadows of

a thousand truths, each deep and mysterious. On impulse, you glance across the lake, and see the High Priestess's temple on the opposite shore. You remember the glimpse you had of this place through her pomegranate curtain. You think to yourself:

A dream that holds my deepest desires is …

You sit by this glistening lake to do some night fishing with your canine companion nestled nearby. Afterwards, you follow the path into the dawn. The Sun rises bright and warm above the hori-  zon. Beneath its glow, a laughing young child on horseback canters toward you. You can't help but be moved by the child's infectious smile. The child jumps off the horse, delighted with the dog's dance of joy. He takes your hand, dragging you off to play. As you bask in the simple joys that bring happiness to the heart of a child, you begin to see the world as the child does. Everything feels possible. There is nothing to be afraid of.

The smiling child asks you:

What are you open to?

Reluctantly, you let the child go and re-  turn to the path. It leads you to a valley of graves. You've hardly decided what to make of it when the angel Gabriel appears in the sky and trumpets a long note on his horn.

The ground beneath you shakes, and you see men, women, and children rising from the graves, holding their arms up to the sky. Gabriel's expression is one of absolute grace. He calls each soul to be redeemed, by the transformative power of love—true Judgement. When his gaze falls upon you, he asks:

To what are you awakening?

You feel full with your life's purpose. You know exactly what it is you are to contribute in this life. Vaguely, you are aware that your journey has brought you back to the cliff's edge where your journey began. Armed with your renewed purpose, you step off the edge of the cliff, and become the World. You say to yourself:

My destiny is…

The dog runs beyond onto another path, but you decide to stay where you are for now.

Each Fool's Journey is unique. Following your heart always leads to new discovery.

Turning Point Exercise 2 might be another way to start making relevant connections in your own Fool's Journey.

Turning Point Exercise 2

Shuffle all your major arcana together. See yourself as the Fool, following your heart and walking down a road. As you travel, direct your steps toward an experience or event in your life. You might take this time to focus particularly on a chapter in your life that was difficult or has not yet been fully resolved. Journey to the moment of change, and visualize that moment, right down to what you were wearing.

Without looking, pick one of the major arcana. Hold that card close to your heart, or any other chakra or energy center where you feel this event lives. Feel the energy of that card and its experience. See if your awareness of that event, that piece of history, changes or shifts at all. Are there any new ideas or thoughts?

Now open your eyes and look at the card. Who is it? How do you feel about the card you selected? Remember the energy you got with your eyes closed and connect it to what you can now see in the card. Does this teacher have more to say to you?

The Essence Spread and Meditation

The time has come to lay the Essence Spread in full. You may use the cards you have already chosen or use the following meditation and do the spread again.

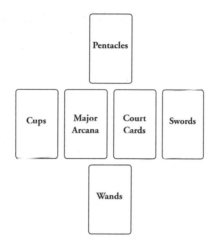

It would be helpful to record the following meditation so that you can play the tape back while doing the spread. We provided the symbol of * for moments to pause while taping. These pauses should span two deep breaths.

Separate the entire deck into the six categories according to the Essence Spread diagram, placing each pile face down in its position to face you.

Close your eyes. Take a few moments to breathe and become fully present in this moment.* Imagine yourself falling, sliding deeper and deeper into yourself.* See yourself in a beautiful, wooded glade at the center of your being. You are alone and feel loose and free. Hear the wind dance through the leaves on the trees. Smell the grass. Feel the warmth of the sun. Taste the cool water of a nearby stream.*

Walk the edges of this glade. Eventually, you will come upon a path. Follow that path deeper into the shaded woods.* You feel a cool breeze. It seems to beckon you to the rocky mouth of a cavern. Know as you stand before the dark that within this cave is your deepest self.*

Enter the cave. Trail your hand along the rough, wet wall. As the darkness engulfs you, you will begin to see images on the walls of the cave. What do you see? What story is being told? * Hold these images in your mind as you journey ahead, spying a tiny light in the darkness.

The light grows brighter with every step you take. Soon, you find yourself in a great, round room.* Walk to the center of this space to the chair prepared for you. It is here that you will call your Divine Committee.

Envision a wide circle of light that surrounds you within this room.* Call into this circle all who protect you, all who are of you. Open the circle for the loving ones that you cannot see. Call the wise advisors from this life and any other. Let them all enter the circle and sit around you.*

When you feel everyone has arrived, whether you can see them distinctly or not, ask your committee a question, or offer them an issue that has been on your mind lately.* Eventually, one of the gathered will approach you. Who is this being to you? What is their wisdom for you?*

The one who came forward moves to stand behind you and places a hand on your shoulder. Concentrate on the being behind you as well as your issue as you turn to the east and pick up your swords group. With your eyes closed, shuffle the swords. As you are shuffling, imagine the morning, the dawn of a new day. Feel the breeze blow through your hair, and smell spring.* The east offers you a gift of a sword. Allow the sword to form in your mind, its type and color. What do the blade and the hilt look like? Once its image stops shifting, and you can clearly see it, draw a card from the swords pile, but don't look at it.* Lay the swords back down in their position with the card you chose flipped face up. Ignore the image for now. Thank the east and move on.

Eyes still closed, turn to the south and wands. Feel the prickling heat of summer on your skin. Pick up the wands group and shuffle. Imagine a desert, wide and beautiful, dry and vast. Fire blazes in its color.* The south offers you a wand, made of a material that sparks your creative spirit. Let the wand dance before you until it has settled on one solid form. Then choose a wand card from the pile.* Without looking, lay the wands back down with your selected card on top. Thank the south for its gift, and turn to the west.

Fall leaves drift down over roaring water. The air is heavy and wet as though after a rain, and the water is refreshingly cold to the touch. Shuffle your cups suit with your eyes closed.* From out of the waters of the west, a chalice appears. It is a wondrous cup, holy and brimming with the nectar of life and emotion. Let the image shift until the cup is real enough to take. Drink from the cup until you are filled, and choose a cup card.* Lay the card on top of its pile without looking at it. Thank the west, and turn north.

Snow-capped mountain peaks fill your vision. It is cold, but in a way that makes you more present in your body. The earth is hard and alive beneath your feet. You feel the potential deep in your bones.* Shuffle the pentacles suit. The north offers you a crystal, stone, or a five-pointed star from the core of earth. When you can see the gift clearly in your mind, draw a pentacle card.* Lay it face up on its pile, but do not look at it. Thank the north for its gift, and focus on the center of your spread.

Pick up your court cards. Shuffle them with your eyes closed, opening your vision to people in your life: people you have met and people you have not.* Ask for the one who influences you most regarding this issue. Once you sense someone, choose the court card that feels right to you.* Lay it on top of its pile without looking at it.

Turn instead to the last stack, the major arcana. Take the cards in hand and shuffle them loosely through your fingertips. Ask the Divine what help or insight it can give you in this situation. Draw the card which has the most energy to the touch.* Set it on top of its pile.

Now open your eyes and allow yourself to see fully. Take in the whole picture before you. What does this look like to you? What connections do you see? What caught your eye first?

Next, begin to read the cards in order starting with the east. What gift did the swords give you? What does it have to do with your issue? What thoughts are needed about this situation? Have any thoughts been holding you back? How can you incorporate this insight or gift into your approach?

Look at the wands. What gift did the south give you? How has your creativity and spirit been dancing with this issue? What potential do you see in this card? What would really spark your passion about this situation? Or does this situation have you burned out?

Now look at the cups. What gift did the west give you? How have you been feeling about this issue? What needs to be nurtured? Is your heart on board with your current approach?

What about the pentacles? What gift did the north give you? What do you physically need for this question to be resolved? What has the north suggested to you to help you fulfill that need? How is your body feeling in regard to the situation?

Go to the center of the circle. Look at the court card you chose. Is this a person you recognize? If so, how is he or she influencing this situation? If you do not know this person, do you get a sense of what role they will play when you meet him or her? Are you surprised by who you chose?

Lastly, look at the Divine energy resting on top of the major arcana. What insight does the Divine offer you? Is this a guide of yours? Is it the one standing with you?

What turning point do you think you are approaching with this issue?

Linger on this spread as long as necessary. Write down everything you think and feel. Read the layers of each card. What symbols stand out to you? What is your immediate reaction? What story do you think this card is telling? See if you can find the challenge and its solution in each one.

When you have gathered what you need to know from the Essence spread, close your eyes once more. See yourself back in the circle of your Divine committee with your guide behind you.* Thank the guide for taking this journey with you. Ask for an image or insight before he or she departs.* Give them a parting gesture, whether it be a hug, a wave, or a simple smile.* Thank your committee for coming, and gently dismiss them so that they may return to their various tasks.

Slowly allow the protective circle around you to dissolve.* Step out of it, out of this place. Follow your cave back to its mouth, paying attention to the walls. Have the images changed? What do you see now?*

Once you are back outside the cave, tilt your head up to the sun. Let its light fill you. Slowly, open your eyes, and come back to this time.

Allow your focus to be soft and hazy as you reorient your surroundings. Remain here until you feel you are firmly in present time. Drinking a glass of water is a splendid habit to develop during and after psychic work.

7

ENERGY BASICS

Perceptions create reality

Now that we've done some tarot exploration, it's time to move on to the basics of reading energy itself. Being able to read energy seems like a magical ability to many observers. It's not. Magical things start to happen when you become conscious of energy, but everyone has the ability to read it. All of us read energy all the time. It's just that most of us only access our intuition or "gut feeling" in times of crisis. The goal of this chapter is to help you become more conscious of energy, to trust your intuitive skills beyond self-preservation.

You read energy every day. When you're picking an apple at the grocery store, you usually choose specific ones from a group. While driving, you're aware of the cars in proximity or even have a sense of their drivers. Most of these are registered on the logical radar long enough to be categorized and then quickly dismissed if no threat is perceived.

Are you aware of any of the ways you already read energy? Do you sometimes know things outside the realm of your five senses? Can you observe without an urge to censor, classify, or minimize? Generally, how are your creative levels? Are you able to sense glimmers of mystery? Do you pay attention to the information you receive "sideways"? For example, while your logical brain is happily "controlling" life, what kinds of quick glimpses of a knowing or a feeling come to you from the side? What is trying to slip in before the censor head files it away? How much of this kind of information do you regularly pass off as your imagination?

Mindfully reading energy comes from the observer within each of us. This gathering of information is done for reasons beyond safety. The observer mind is curious as a cat. The ability to perceive an essence, detect a pattern, catch interesting details, or make connections where there were none a minute before is a pleasurable process with no goal in mind. In this state of awareness, we use our senses to see outside the box. Free from assumed outcomes, we open vision on all levels to see what really exists rather than what our logical mind thinks *should* exist. This demands the ability to hold mysterious clues, ideas, and messages that don't or won't make sense until a whole picture appears. Make peace with the idea that what you sense may not *make* sense. It is more important that the information be true than logical or "right."

We tend to dismiss what we can't quantify. Information you did not hear, see, smell, or touch is hard to trust.

Our logic demands tangible proof. It takes some practice to get comfortable with the idea that your whole being receives valuable data. You only need to figure out how you switch off the inner censor in order to pay attention to the observer within.

Allow for some awkwardness as you learn how to shift the logical to the creative. Eventually, both will be needed when reading energy, but the observer needs to come first. Initially, you might feel like Alice going down the rabbit hole or through the looking glass. Like Alice, your curiosity will be piqued when you glimpse the unusual. Trying to catch the mystery will involve an entire journey at times. This adventure of strange clues and odd messages will necessitate leaving old perceptions behind. In reading energy, you need to open your mind as well as your heart. The observer within each of us is always game!

To discover this observer within, gently challenge your habitual ways of perception. A simple way of receiving information that goes beyond the rational five senses is to simply close your eyes. Sight becomes *in*-sight. Imagine a blank movie screen or curtains slowly opening onto a stage. Allow reality to dance, play, and show you unseen truths. As you think of a particular event or situation, see what characters appear. What feelings or stories is the Creative Unknown sending? Can you see a deeper or secret truth? Rather than a tidy linear story, expect glimpses and flashes of insight. It may seem strange, but the information will appear to you in ways you can embrace.

Another exercise to strengthen observational skills is practicing on other people. In loving curiosity, use public environments—such as the bank or waiting in line at a store—to test new ways of perception that tend to be wholly unconscious. Go beyond your rational "sizing up" to sense the essences of people nearby. Who are their ancestors? Can you imagine their past lives? What do you perceive as their basic elemental nature: fiery, fluid, grounded, or airy? Different questions yield different perceptions.

Sometimes you might even sense a response to energy in your body. For instance, the timbre of a person's voice can ignite a certain reaction. If they're speaking of their own physicality and you have a sense of tightness somewhere in your body, you may be accessing their energetic story. As you listen to someone speak on the radio, can you imagine how they look or dress? Often, asking creative questions provokes vision.

There's a wealth of information hidden everywhere; start to become a joyful excavator! Powerful connections often come as a response to the question "What do I need to know?" Invisible details emerge once you start to trust seeing and hearing and sensing differently. Move more freely in the gray area. You will find that things aren't always as they appear.

Magic is found in the mundane. One will need an artist-like curiosity and confidence to envision new worlds of possibilities. In a state of clear sight, new connections make themselves known. Let's try this sense of seeing.

Mystery Images

This one is fun to do with friends. Go through magazines or old books and cut out fifteen or twenty images. Put each one in its own envelope, preferably identical and opaque. Shuffle the envelopes until you cannot tell which envelope holds which image.

Take about fifteen minutes to sense how each concealed image is speaking to you in terms of energy by simply holding each envelope. You may sense very literal images such as numbers or names. Write on each envelope any trigger of feeling received. The information you receive does not have to make sense or be consistent, and you're not trying to guess what's in each envelope. Relax and receive without doubt. Let go of the perfectionist within—it doesn't belong in spirit space.

Afterwards, open each envelope to see what is inside. Do you notice any pattern or connections between the images and what you wrote about them? Is there any relevance to the messages received? See if you can start to connect ideas with energy, images with words, and how you connect the dots. Pay little attention to labels of "right" or "wrong."

So how does one interpret all these connections and the energy clues gathered? It's very much like the TV series *Columbo*. The central character was a detective who always seemed slightly confused and not very organized, but somehow he caught information others trivialized or missed altogether. Like that clever detective, patiently wait for a message to form itself. Release the need for action until you receive clear marching orders.

Remember, while sifting through information you need to take the risk of being wrong or inconsistent. Mystery isn't at your beck and call. It reveals itself in its own time and in its own way.

P EOPLE ASK ME HOW ACCURATE I AM. My REPLY IS, "I AM MORE ACCURATE THAN MOST METEOROLOGISTS, THOUGH I AM DOING THE SAME THING: I RECOGNIZE THE STORM FRONTS AND TELL THE POSSIBLE TEMPERATURE FOR THE DAY, BUT NEVER REALLY KNOW WHAT THE GREATER UNIVERSE MIGHT HAVE IN MIND."

Following is a variation of an exercise designed by Echo Bodine, a nationally known psychic and author. It will strengthen your resolve to be true rather than accurate.

Dead or Alive Exercise

Find a partner or someone who is willing to let you read for them. Ask them to focus on someone they love dearly, whether that person is presently alive or not. Have your partner write that person's name down (but not let you see it). Answer the following six questions without any help from your partner.

1. Is this person dead or alive?

2. Is this person female or male?

3. Is this person light-skinned or dark?

4. What age does this person appear to be to you?

5. Is this person skinny, average, or heavy?

6. What message does this loved one have for your partner?

Check your answers with your partner. You aren't going to be right all the time. You may not even be right half the time. The point of this exercise is to evaporate those fears of not being right and gain confidence in making connections.

The goal of mindfully sensing the essence of people, stories, events, or even the future is to be true rather than rational. Taking this first step can be tricky, but the dance that will evolve between you and the Creative Unknown is worth it!

Another exercise to strengthen your energy perception is to start a synchronicity journal.

Synchronicity

Start a new journal or dedicate a large section of your tarot journal to spotting instances of synchronicity. Note all daily moments of it. For example, note the times you were thinking of a person and they call you, or you've really wanted to read a certain book and someone just happens to give it to you. Simply wanting to record synchronicity will encourage more of it to happen. It is an invitation for the observer within each of us to come out and play.

8

Seeing the Unseen

*In clear sight, our world
and the world beyond are one*

As we embark on our journey of using our senses differently, beliefs regarding the unseen worlds will become increasingly influential. What have you come to believe about ghosts, gods, angels, and other invisible beings? What source sustains you in times of crisis? Where do you return repeatedly to nourish your connection to your life? Which concepts have remained or evolved from your early training? With a renewed clarity, these inner convictions will serve as your compass in navigating new worlds.

The pulse of this work is Creative Authority, the expression of one's life with full acceptance of one's own loving nature. The source of our very being is spirit. Accepting both our human and spirit selves helps us become truly real. All creativity flows from this connection.

Unfortunately, many of us have a broken connection. We learned that love comes with conditions and rules, actually diminishing love's power. Creative authority is believing in your own worth to love and be loved, warts and all.

You may also have learned that what one cannot see or touch should be feared: anything of magical quality is deemed safe only through religious middle management. Or perhaps you may have learned that going straight to the source would create imbalance, beckoning forces that will consume you or make you crazy. The last trace of magical invisible worlds disappeared for most of us as children. Entire worlds of beings, expression, and creativity became inaccessible when we surrendered to others' authority on love.

It is essential to declare your own Creative Authority by exploring your true reality regarding life, death, and everything in between. What is your reason for being here? How do you express your life? How can you fully express yourself as human and spirit? On your last day, what would you like to have accomplished? What do you need to do to release those teachings that prevent you from exploring love without fear?

If this review of your belief system seems too daunting, consider the idea that all energy is either love or fear. You can serve one or the other, but not both at the same time. Believing this may open new doors for even the most mundane decision you need to make. Ask yourself, "Is this intent based in love, or in fear?" Strong intention makes for strong decisions.

Not only is your own authority required, but a different kind of sight is needed due to the spirit realm's invisible nature. Learning ways to perceive, understand, and communicate with that which you cannot see will hopefully reduce the "weird" factor of what you experience!

Let's begin with the major source of energy. Although many of us learned this source can only be Divine, it can just as well be your higher self, the Creative Unknown, pure energy, a great spirit, or perhaps nature. What source of love would you serve? What forms other than humans would love create?

Humans certainly are not the only perceivable manifestation of love. Invisible beings exist as well, though they need to be perceived in a different manner. Among the beings that may make an appearance in our lives, angels, ghosts, spirits, ancestors, and psyche selves are frequent visitors.

Consider that each of us is a spirit who decided to have a human adventure. We are each given our own Divine support system to help us remember our spirit connection in spite of what seems to be our separation from the source.

Life isn't necessarily defined by inhabiting a body or not! Anyone who has lost someone dear most certainly experiences the "spirit" of the departed's life and essence. In fact, some spirits seem more alive than those of us who are actually shuffling through life.

Saying a loved one's name out loud greatly helps you to sense the person. It aids in creating a reality for things our eyes cannot see. Once their name is spoken, there may be a heightened sense of their essence, like someone entering a room. Another facet of creating a new communication is creating a system so the departed can initiate contact with you. Asking a deceased loved one to visit you during dreams helps maintain an open dialogue.

A FTER MY BEST FRIEND DENNIS DIED, WE SET UP A SYSTEM. IF I HEAR ONE OF OUR FIVE FAVORITE DANCE SONGS, I SAY, "DENNIS, WHAT'S UP?" I KNOW HE IS CALLING ME.

It's a good idea to allow a three- to six-month grace period before actively trying to contact someone who has recently died; loss is a powerful state of being. The first stage of grief can involve deep sorrow, loneliness, and even numbness. Let that initial cycle pass before contacting your loved one beyond the veil.

A common request during a tarot reading is for a message from a departed parent or other loved one. In many circumstances, spirits of a loved one are quite willing to come and give counsel. They are still engaged in love and awareness of those living.

One client of mine wanted to speak to her father. What she wasn't fully aware of was that she'd already been communicating with him since his death. For instance, a few days after the funeral, she felt silly for the first time since he had gotten ill and passed. For a brief moment, she felt like she was joking with him, but it seemed odd to feel joy.

Another time, at the grocery store, she passed jars of peppers which made her think of the Italian meals he used to cook and it made her ache for him. Later that evening, a neighbor bought over a handful of peppers fresh from her garden.

I asked her father to visit us. After silently asking and pulling a few cards, I was aware of a presence off to the side of the room. I used my inner eyes to see an image of a stocky, older man standing there with his arms crossed over his chest. He seemed surprised to see her at a tarot reading. Internally, I said, "Hello. I know this may seem strange, but I know you are here. If you would give me any messages for your daughter, she will be well served by it."

He told me of things and people that helped his daughter sense his presence such as the silliness after his funeral and the peppers. He mentioned her oldest brother by name, spoke of their family farm, and counseled her about some things her mother would need. She jumped in recognition of his references and a few specific phrases. He acknowledged both times that she had indeed sensed him. She felt relieved to not have lost all contact with him. Her intuitive sensing of him would now grow in confidence and the sorrow wasn't as overwhelming with this knowledge.

Sensing a presence nearly always enters your awareness in a sideways manner. The focus and gaze needs to be soft and receptive. You might think of it like fishing: you throw out the line and patiently wait. Often there is a small tug, sometimes a direct pull. If you sense some of this sideways activity or a small tug during a reading, simply ask the presence for its identity and purpose. A spirit will almost always show a very clear image of who they are. This reflection may be exactly how they looked in life. Sometimes you will be given just a name or a characteristic such as smoking or a particular perfume. The dialogue with a spirit is usually loving, uplifting, and even humorous at times.

Spirits don't dwell on their death and they often steer the seeker from that final chapter as well. The focus is nearly always on shared love—fond memories, courageous moments, or even future events such as births or other additions to the family. Spirits come when they are needed, which doesn't always mean they come when called. They always leave when they are done; we don't hold spirits.

Like spirits, ghosts also had human lives. They have not crossed over to the source of love. They are still attached to their former bodies and egos for various reasons, and do not want to cross over. They frequently make very little sense and are primarily focused on their own needs. They tend to repeat the same ideas and thoughts. The atmosphere will often be tense or weird. Ghosts stubbornly refuse to yield any relevant information. They rarely show up at a reading, but it is helpful to know when one might be present. The only communication needed for a ghost is telling it to go to the light or elsewhere!

Of course, some ghosts who have recently passed over haven't formed an intent to stay on this plane, and are genuinely confused. They could use a little prodding from those they trust.

> *One morning after arriving at the office, I found out that a co-worker had died the night before from a heart attack. A few days later, most of the office was closed so we could attend his wake and funeral.*
>
> *I went into the office beforehand to finish a few tasks. The feeling of the office was strange. No one else was there. I enjoyed the rare silence as I sorted and dropped off mail to different cubicles.*
>
> *It slowly dawned on me that I wasn't alone as I walked down an aisle heading towards John's desk. I suddenly realized he was working in his cubicle, oblivious to any change! I thought I was imagining things, but I made myself say aloud, "John, honey, you've died. You need to go the funeral soon." Then, thinking of what I would really say to John if he were alive, I added, "Don't worry, you won't miss this job."*
>
> *I was shocked when this image responded immediately to my words. At first he seemed confused, but then he smiled—something had clicked. The vision drifted away like a dream upon waking.*
>
> *At the funeral, I felt grateful to be a small help in his orientation as I saw him stand behind his wife, his hands on her shoulders.*

There are spirits or ghosts of another category altogether. Anyone who committed suicide is markedly different than other departed humans. These souls seem to undergo rehabilitation on the other side. Suicides generally won't show up at a reading unless they've reached the point of understanding their final action. Though they are still in a "therapy" stage, they may still be able to send messengers or guides with comforting information to their loved ones.

Ancestors are our particular "clan" of spirits. Not only are they sources of our DNA and blood, they also carry certain spiritual patterns as well. During a reading, these spiritual themes might be experienced as an irrefutable sense of a way of being in the world or specific rules of living, loving, and working. Much of our reality is shaped by our parents. When these realities need to shift, it is helpful to go to the ancestors, since they make up the long line of beliefs passed from one generation to the next. Addictions, alcoholism, and physical vulnerabilities can be traced (in the spiritual realm) to an ancestor who made a decision in fear for survival. You can call on ancestor energy to unravel patterns and ways of living that have become destructive.

Bathtub Meditation

A simple technique for reaching your spiritual ancestors can be done in the safety and leisurely timing of a nice hot bath. After you are relaxed and quiet in the water, visualize your mother, her mother, and her mother all the way back to the beginning of your gene pool. Walk past each one until you sense the one woman who is the source of your current fear or dysfunction. If you can see her face, ask her to tell you her story. Why did this start? What were her choices? Tell her how the issue has manifested itself in your life. Ask her to help release you from this grip. This can be done with your father and his family issues too.

A comfortable invisible being for most is the angel. There is evidence of angelic beings that predate Judeo-Christian religions. Helpful, winged creatures were depicted in the ancient art of Mesopotamia, Greece, and Egypt, among others. Most religions today have angels and it seems as if they represent the library of invisible beings. Angels appear when specifically requested. You may not have consciously called one, but perhaps you've experienced a sense of grace during a crisis—a sure sign one has come to your aid. An angel feels like love, pure and simple. Their presence speaks volumes.

So who guides your spirit? What would your guide or guides look like? Call a conference to discover your spiritual co-creators! Take a few minutes to play with this concept of the "Divine committee." Let your focus go within. Release any cynicism, fear, or pain from old teachings. Open to a loving source that nourishes and strengthens your heart and mind. Visualize a place to gather, such as at a conference table or around a fire. Open to the greatest amount of love you can imagine. Who would join you? Who do you hope to see? This is your committee.

> M Y CURRENT COMMITTEE IS BUDDHA, JESUS, BRIGIT, A WHITE STAG, AND SOME RABBITS.

The human experience is that of a pioneer, a rugged adventure with cruel limitations and sublime freedoms. It culminates in the love we give and take. Each of us has our own Divine committee that helps us stay connected to the true source of love during our brief journey on earth. This connection allows us to fully experience being both human and spirit in this present moment.

9

THE MANY SELVES

Each soul is a constellation

The psyche selves are a group of invisibles that have significant information about and for the seeker. These selves are literally parts of one's unconscious, representing aspects of the personality. Often these are the seeker's strong needs and desires. The separateness of some of these aspects creates the illusion of each having a personality of its own.

Often, the seeker is well aware of unresolved needs and suppressed talents. What he or she may not know is how all of these blocks and limitations came to be, and where potential is hiding. It can be shocking to hear of the exact event that resulted in an emotional paralysis or a belief that spurred a rigid censor. Using the psyche selves format, the reader can be well advised by the seeker him- or herself, indirectly!

It is as if the seeker were the director of a large, colorful cast of actors. Each represents a role the seeker plays, such as the artist, the daughter, the lover, etc. Each psyche self holds a specific gift, strength, and vulnerability that may not be integrated into the whole persona.

When dealing with psyche selves, the reader is the negotiator between the psyche self and the seeker. The goal is to raise the seeker's awareness of her whole being by focusing on relevant needs and skills that may be otherwise undermined or ignored completely. When relating this dialogue to the seeker, you may be met with either utter bewilderment or instant recognition. The reading is an opportune time to find new insights to break down the walls of rigidity or fear.

A psyche self takes form when directly asked compassionate questions such as:

Why did you develop?

How old are you?

What is your need?

What part of the story is yours?

What role do you play on the seeker's team?

What will you need in order to go along with the seeker's goals?

If that need cannot be fulfilled at this time, what would you be willing to accept in trade?

It may sound like a strange way to call out a part of
a person, but it works! The psyche self shows an aspect
of the seeker not integrated into the whole. Such aspects
can be stories of hurt, neglect, or anger. The psyche self
often protects the big self, which translates into the act of
compartmentalizing particular thoughts and feelings. As
such, there is often great creativity and power released in
these negotiations.

To dialogue with a psyche self is a way to release anxiety,
illusions, and unconscious reactions in making choices. To
personify fear gives one the chance to truly converse and
listen with one's heart. The appearance and temperament
of each psyche self is the telltale message in most cases.
If, for instance, the seeker wants some clarification on the
lack of progress in his career as an engineer, the reader
might be served to ask for any psyche self that has strong
opinions on money and work.

Dialogue with the seeker's psyche selves might go
something like this: the reader closes his or her eyes and
silently calls a conference of the seeker's psyche selves.
When it feels like "everyone" who was going to show up
has shown up, the reader asks for the psyche self blocking
the seeker's progress in his or her career life, for example,
to come forward. A farmer appears. When asked why he
stands in opposition to the seeker's goal, he replies that he
only trusts what he can grow. This exploration with the
seeker may be served by questions such as "Have you ever
wanted to be a farmer?" "Do you think your work serves
a purpose?" "Would you rather be on your own than in

a team?" "What are you trying to grow with your work?" Come up with a few new and creative strategies based on the seeker's input. If nothing else, suggest the seeker approach work in the manner of a farmer.

The most important facet of this method is revealing the leader of all of these needs. If any aspect of the personality is given full power, the balance is off. Who has the power? The controlling censor? A scared eight-year-old? Simply asking who has the power is a surprisingly effective technique in gathering information. This is an internal dialogue you as a reader would then discuss with the seeker. If the naysayer is managing all the other needs, for example, you would inform the seeker of a great need to resist listening to the censor within. Another example would be the wounded child running the show. Your creative suggestion as a consultant might give the seeker the idea to assume the full powers of his or her true age and let the little one go play with the fairies (which should have happened when the seeker was an actual child).

Psyche selves can also be personified needs from past lives. Often, irrational fears can be pinned to a psyche self with unresolved past-life experiences. Gather some clues to discover the influential past life. What is your favorite era? What do you like to study? Are you drawn to a certain geographical location or civilization? What kinds of music make you weep? Is there a manner of dying you fear more than anything? The way you fear death may come from actually having experienced it in a past life. Rather than navel-gazing, exploring your past lives can short-circuit a lot of fears and resistance that keep you from fully loving this life.

The more you listen to each need as its own person, the more you learn what is needed for the whole person. Everyone wants something, so use this knowledge to the seeker's advantage. The following story may help to illustrate this idea.

I was unable to conceive a child. When I went deep within, I found an irrational fear of dying during labor. I spoke to that fear as if she were a person. I had the distinct impression she was me from a past life. I had obviously died during labor, and had no desire to go through the experience again.

But I wanted the son I had seen in visions past. So I asked this psyche self, "What could I do to help you, so that you will help me become pregnant and won't stand in my way?" She answered, "Scotland." So off I went.

While there, I received a detailed story. I realized that this was the land of that unfortunate death. During that life, I evidently got pregnant from the wrong man and was shunned by my clan. I died trying to deliver my baby alone. My past-life psyche wanted to see Scotland one more time before she "died again." With all those deaths behind me, I returned home, and conceived my son.

Unheard or unacknowledged needs will find ways to be heard in sometimes unpleasant ways: some may become quite disruptive or cause an energetic stalemate. Can you visualize your group of psyche selves? Which ones have a gripe? How are you as the leader? Is every vote being counted? Have you exiled anyone? Being the Creative Authority requires careful negotiation of these inner landscapes.

10

TRUSTING THE SIGHT

In a rich silence, all can be heard

A common inner landscape many tarot readers visit again and again in meditation is the temple of the High Priestess, which traditionally sits before a moonlit sea. The High Priestess and the Moon cards are really opposite sides of the same "place" in the tarot quest. Sitting in her temple with the veil behind her, the High Priestess is quite literally guarding the secrets of the Moon. If you were to step into the High Priestess card and venture just beyond the veil, you would find yourself standing in the Moon card. The High Priestess is symmetrical, orderly, approachable, intuitive, helpful, and wise. She holds in her hand your life's scroll (that wonderful to-do list we'd all like to read) and can always produce just the knowledge you need for any given situation. As a reader, you might aspire to be like her. She's a very good guide.

Stepping into your psychic self is sometimes like stepping past the High Priestess's veil and into the Moon.

The Moon is mysterious and chaotic, and tends to distort things or enshroud them in shadow. All knowledge is there like the vast ocean. Your ability to master your Moon side while standing right in it, rather than keeping it safely behind the veil, is a very important part of reading cards intuitively.

But first, your intuition needs to be developed. This process happens in small increments of trust. Finding your unique vision and voice is the foundation of trust. Later in this book are chapters describing the six principles, a step-by-step method to enter a reading in a deeper, more directed way. Before taking that path, however, it is important to strengthen your confidence.

Divination is the art of finding the most profound, relevant question behind all other questions. A great question practically contains the answer itself! The core question is the one that lights up the greatest number of psychic light bulbs, so to speak. It has the greatest power to shine a light on an important issue or idea. The very first question or need for clarification is often the first veil to deeper levels of awareness. The authentic question is surfaced through a process of honest and practical introspection. We will explore the makings of a great question in chapter 13, about intent.

A relevant reading begins with entering spirit space. Spirit space is a process of "becoming your spirit," the release of attachments or ego. This place of nonjudgment and compassion opens a world of possibilities and potential where your Moon self becomes accessible. Your question or intent will serve as your compass.

One enters this space by shedding all desired outcomes. Only then can one stand in a new awareness of choices. The linear mind becomes more neutral, calm, and spacious. Controlled breathing, meditation, and visualization are prime techniques to move from "human" time into spirit space.

It takes practice and experimentation to find a comfortable level in stillness. Many are uncomfortable with meditation or the absence of stimulation. Start small to develop these psychic muscles. Use a timer, starting with five minutes. Sit quietly and be still. Let go of the world. Release all your responsibilities and all the things that are calling for your attention and focus. Feel a space where you are centered and free from everyday preoccupations. Over time, gradually increase the minutes. Those who practice gain the confidence and expansion of a quiet mind and trusting heart.

After some degree of stillness has been achieved, the receptivity switch can be considered "on." At this point, you will be gathering knowledge. There is no pressure to act on any information received. Let the insight flow in. The new "knowings" will come like birds to a tree.

All of this requires a level of trust. Trusting the connection to a greater source is the biggest step of trust. What do you connect to in order to find that greater potential? Is it God? Is it Love? Is it the Creative Unknown or your higher self? Could you believe in the concept of co-creating your life with a Divine committee? If unsure, concentrate on those times in this life when you experienced so much joy, you felt as though you were nearly transported from this world into another. Occasions when you've "lost time" are a source of creative passion. Trust those memories while recreating a spacious sanctuary within.

The following are some exercises to help strengthen your trust in your Sight.

The Destiny Self

You will need paper, a pencil or pen, and perhaps some markers or crayons. Sit down with the supplies in front of you. Use whatever method works best for you to enter spirit space. Breathe to relax.

Imagine yourself on the last day of your life, an older version of yourself who has completely manifested this life's destiny. Listen quietly as this future self appears. Ask this future self what you need to be on your path of authentic living or what may be needed to change your current direction.

For the next fifteen minutes, just scribble or color. Put on music, if it helps. Just let the insight flow through your hands. Be very free with this time. Remain open to receive a response through a message or image.

At the end of the fifteen minutes, if you didn't receive any ideas, images, or knowledge of some sort, go to whatever book you're drawn to in the room you're in. Open a page and point. The Sight works beautifully through synchronicity in the natural world.

I HAVE ASKED MY DIVINE COMMITTEE TO
PRESENT THREE BIRDS TOGETHER IF IT IS
TIMELY TO MEDITATE FOR INSIGHT.

Hidden Questions Exercise

This exercise will require three sheets of paper, blank envelopes, and a writing instrument. Focus on three different questions or intents that have been on your radar screen lately. Attempt to hone the questions until they are very specific. Write each on a sheet of paper, fold, and seal individually in the envelopes. If you can't think of any questions immediately, you could always rely on the three general areas of career, love, and health. The envelopes should be indistinguishable from each other once sealed.

Every day for a week, after a five-minute meditation, write onto each envelope any hit or trigger you get from simply holding it. Rate each trigger or symbol received on a scale of 10 to 1. Ten is a spot-on intuitive hit. One is a wild guess. Five would indicate some ambiguity of the two extremes. Don't judge or change the information; record the insights as completely and honestly as possible.

After a week, open the envelopes. Read each question in light of all its received messages. Any surprises? After absorbing some of the ideas, look at the triggers marked 10. Were they more relevant? How about those rated 1? Were any of the wild guesses applicable?

The Sideways Exercise

When developing Sight, synchronicity becomes your new best friend. Record a question or need for clarification about a specific area in your life. Put it aside for an hour or so. During that time, make sure your receptivity switch is "on." Go for a walk or engage in an activity that promotes observation, such as sitting by a window. Pay attention to all events as if you were living in a time zone of synchronicity. What catches your attention or focus? Briefly note every event in the order they occur.

After the specified time, look at the list of received messages as if it were a secret response to your question that you need to decode. As with dream imagery, write down the first thing that comes to your mind for each message or event. This does not have to be rational as much as it should ring true to you.

Read aloud the interpreted messages from beginning to end, as when reading a book. Hopefully, a myth-like story will emerge. For example:

I went for a walk. I saw a V formation of geese flying south. A mother walked past with a child fussing loudly. I enjoyed the whiff of baking bread somewhere nearby.

Would become:

When it is time to change the direction of my life, I can feel the support of others. I am not alone. Change does tend to make me cranky, however. I need to remember that the basics of life—good food and good friends—will help me.

Or:

I saw a plane draw an X in the sky and a young woman who resembled my departed Aunt Nellie. She smiled broadly at me.

Would become:

Aunt Nellie sends her love and tells me to enjoy being a young woman.

So how did the story you receive shift your original question? Does it offer specific answers or does it lead you in an entirely different direction? Noticing a larger, hidden reality where everything is connected opens our abilities to receive pure magic.

Part of learning to use the Sight is the desire to read for others. In this relationship it is important to have a clear idea of your role. Many names have been assigned to this role—psychic, medium, channeler, advisor, or seer—but they are all governed by the first and most important role: witness. To witness in this sense is to listen with an open heart and quiet mind. It is an act of respecting the boundaries of integrity, personal safety, and loving empathy.

Imagine every person on this planet healing to the best of his or her abilities. When we serve as witnesses to each other, we promote love and awareness. The people who come to your doorstep are ready to hear and, more importantly, ready to speak. You are there as their witness and should not underestimate what they know about themselves, their lives, or their potential for growth. Your job is to create a sacred space for people to share and to realize their truths.

Always be prepared for tears, anger, fear, and shock. It may be hard to let oneself be truly seen or heard. Emotions are an organic byproduct of truth. It isn't your job to fix or change anyone; your job is to offer engaged silence as a mindful witness who can receive messages from a greater source of love.

I ASSURE THE CLIENT THAT TEARS CAN BE VERY HELPFUL. I REFER TO THEM AS "TAROT TEARS." AS WITH LAUGHTER, TEARS ARE POTENT ENOUGH TO BREAK UP OLD PATTERNS.

There will be more about boundaries later, but there are a couple of things you should know right from the start. A reading is an act of trust. Much like a doctor, therapist, or lawyer, there is a code of confidentiality. Even in a professional support setting with a trusted peer, refrain from using names.

Also, while you are a novice reader, resist being tested. There are people who visit psychics with the intent of testing their accuracy. Psychic work is a collaborative process, not a firing line. In some respects, it demands not only a suspension of disbelief on your part, but also on behalf of the person working with you.

As a novice reader, practice reading for people who support your intuitive skills. You might also want to explain the reading process beforehand. For instance, it would help them to know that you may want to close your eyes. That seems like such a simple thing, but in our culture it can be awkward. This action can be a powerful way to shift energy. Perhaps you will scribble. It works very well to aid the flow of information. Simple descriptions of your process will enhance the comfort level for both the reader and the seeker during a reading.

When working with another, offer a short verbal intent for both of you to release the pressures and responsibilities of modern living to create spirit space together. If your seekers seem comfortable with the idea, suggest they close their eyes and breathe slowly as they sense their calm center.

I OFTEN DO GROUNDING EXERCISES WITH MY CLIENTS. I SUGGEST THAT THE WORLD WILL CALMLY WAIT OUTSIDE THE DOOR FOR THEM.

Taking small steps in trusting your own intuitive language is often strengthened when shared with another.

11

❦

The Initial Image

Moving in Divine will

A good way to get your intuitive compass pointing north during a reading is to seek out an initial image. The initial image is like no other technique proposed by other tarot readers. It is ideally suited for reading using psychic tarot in that one receives a psychic message or image before reading any cards. It is a quickly flashed image of the seeker at the moment of the reading. This could be received as a short movie, a picture, or simply a knowing of the seeker as their souls would have us know. The image or story clarifies the seeker's current relationships with their own lives and goes beyond any symptoms they might initially present. Capturing the state of the seeker's mind or spirit is profoundly useful when seeking the right tone or direction for the reading.

Finding the initial image isn't very complicated: simply close your eyes, open your intuitive channels, and quietly ask the Creative Unknown for a story relating to the seeker's soul. The process may feel a bit like hide-and-seek: you ask to see the soul's story and then attempt to locate the seeker.

Note that you won't always receive an initial image. The request for one is only granted when necessary to inform the reading.

When given, initial images often appear as short films. For instance, the seeker is on a roller coaster or running down a country road with others. Other times it may be just a snapshot, such as a worried king on his throne or a young child looking at frog eggs. Most of the time, this is a "knowing," meaning that you don't really see anything as much as sense a story that proceeds in your imagination as if you were creating it. But you are *not* creating it, you are receiving it. The difference is the sacred intent, which will be explained more fully within the Six Principles system.

Explore the initial image method for yourself. Find a willing partner for this exercise.

The Initial Image Evocation

Before much dialogue with your partner, close your eyes and internally ask for a story or a small movie that illustrates this person's current state of being. Questions that might trigger this image are: What is most influencing the person right now? What past-life issue, if any, is being worked out? Do you detect any healing? How does your partner like being on this planet? Who is he or she right now? What do I need to know right now to give as good a reading as possible? What does this person need to understand at this time?

You may receive a scene as brief and seemingly unrelated as the person picking berries on a mountain or walking a tightrope while blindfolded. The image can be very fairy tale–like or starkly real. Breathe and be receptive to an image or story that vividly describes the seeker's current reality. Describe this vision to your partner. Discuss any trigger this may have, if any.

Ask which area or issue of your partner's life could use different insight. As you listen to the response, keep in mind the initial image's energy. Look behind words where bigger questions often hide. Ask more questions about the person's question. "Is this what you really want to know?" or "I'm sensing something behind it, could that be the true matter?" Track and trust any variety of intuitive hit you get.

Once you both agree on the core question, close your eyes. Think of that initial soul story. Did the story shed light on the questions? Did the questions shed light on the story? For the next ten minutes or so, tell your partner your new sense of the story. If you received any kind of knowledge, pass it along, even if you don't understand it. Speak of the messages without apology, censorship, or immediate validation. It's important to let information flow unfettered. Afterwards, ask if this made sense or possibly triggered something deeper.

The initial image is a powerful first nod from the source. Even if the information received from this spiritual snapshot detours from the seeker's main focus, its direction is the one to follow.

For instance, let's say the initial image of a particular seeker portrays her joyfully singing onstage. When asked what brings her to the reading, however, she is intently focused on solutions for her unhappy marriage! As a reader, you would certainly explore the different dimensions of the marriage. But the Creative Unknown has given a significant clue for the focus of the reading, something about her creativity, her voice, or acknowledgment. Would a focus on her creativity serve both her and the marriage? What does she want to sing about? Could she be distracting herself with the relationship rather than stepping up to the plate with her own life risks? The reason for the image may not be clear in the beginning, but it remains a relevant clue—it's spiritual information calling for recognition.

You may or may not disclose the image you receive to the seeker, but certainly relate it when deemed important. For example, consider an initial image of a seeker flying in a hot air balloon, enjoying the scenery below. This doesn't give you much to go on, so you progress with the reading, keeping the image in the back of your mind. You become acutely aware of a pattern of noncommitment as the reading progresses. The seeker's choices seem to show a tendency to stay aloof, to not handle things well on the ground. The initial image illustrates a need to be far above the ground. You suggest exploring the person's views of commitment by asking, "What would be the worst-case scenario of staying in one place or one relationship for many years?" or "Do you enjoy watching life from afar?" "When was the last time you really felt grounded?"

Finding the true challenge or question reaps great insights. The initial image may have invaluable information to get to the heart of the matter. Deeper values surface, are examined, and are possibly shifted. To paraphrase Anton Chekhov when he spoke of storytellers, it's not your job to solve the problem—it is to state it clearly.

12

THE FIRST PRINCIPLE: GROUNDING

To grow well, we need to feel our roots

The next several chapters will demonstrate the Six Principles, a system useful for any kind of divination. These principles are Grounding, Intent, Form, Synchronicity, Closure, and Integration. Tarot is, of course, the featured sacred tool. Let us begin with Grounding.

As an astronaut exploring space, you'd first establish a link between your shuttle and the space center's control team. The purpose of grounding is to approach reading while connected to the Divine. Because no reading is casual, every time you use the Sight, it is imperative you connect to a greater source of love. Hold strong and clear boundaries, clarity of thought and feeling, and a sense of movement and growth. These things should be considered whether you are reading for yourself or others.

The first essential step in Grounding is a willingness to suspend your perceptions and projections. Become as clear-sighted as possible. The destination is hearing, seeing, and sensing from your heart, soul, and mind. This is not an attempt to create a state of holiness, but rather a state of being truly present.

To enter spirit time, the second necessary step is to leave the censor behind. The censor is very helpful during the day, but in sacred time becomes chatter. It's important to learn how to switch off and minimize it to curtail second-guessing and doubt.

This altered state of consciousness is one of active listening. In lay terms, *stop talking*. As a novice, there is almost a guarantee of initial discomfort in yielding control. Reassure the busy part of your brain that you are simply exploring other ways of thinking, and if you like, find playful ways to negotiate your inner power struggle between the logical and the intuitive.

I OFTEN SEE MY CHATTER MIND AS THE DUCHESS WITH THE ROLLING PIN IN *Alice in Wonderland*. I SHRINK HER TO ABOUT HALF AN INCH TALL, SO THAT EVEN THOUGH SHE IS STILL THERE, I DON'T HAVE TO LISTEN TO HER.

There are many ways to Ground, a few of which are listed here. Most Grounding is composed of some sort of rhythmic (slow, deep) breathing, closed eyes, and shifting your focus inward. One approach is to honor your everyday efforts; gratitude is a wonderful chariot to ride into spirit space. Close your eyes and acknowledge entirely your efforts and focus. Reevaluate how you're dealing with adversity in your life. Don't judge these efforts—simply observe with kindness. Acknowledge the pressures of your expectations and responsibilities. Go deep into a place of gratitude, breathe, and release it all.

Another type of grounding is noticing and releasing any current blocks or resistances. Inwardly scan your body, mind, and heart. What are your biggest complaints or aches right now? Breathe into those areas. Resist the need to fix or judge—simply acknowledge and bless them as a part of living. Again, remember that breathing is a helpful action that releases and relaxes.

Breath is your reliable transport from "human" time to spirit time, and there are all kinds of techniques. Find methods that help you let go of your thoughts, such as sending breath to your lungs, belly, and feet. Breath grounds the spirit in the body where it can freely function as, say, a radio signal.

Visualization is also a useful tool for those of us who think in pictures. For instance, see all the current actions and efforts you put out in the world as a beautiful spiral that swirls gracefully around you instead of within you. Intensify this method by viewing this spiral as your favorite color. Hold on to nothing. Let go of any attachments to any past efforts, send them out to the spiral, and trust in this moment that all will be well.

Another way of Grounding, for those who have an interest in chakras, is to pull cleansing energy into you, from crown to root. Chakras are the energy wheels believed to be housed in different parts of your body. The seven major wheels form a vertical line from the top of your head to the apex of your legs (pelvis). Hold the cards at crown level and "pull" them all the way down through your energy wheels, through crown, third eye, throat, heart, solar plexus, sacral, and root. Do this three times. The first time, envision both you and your deck emptying all attachments. Become an empty vessel. On the second pass, imagine white light filling you and the deck. Use the third pass to seal that blank energy into you and the deck for the duration of the reading. This method encourages your chakras to be unified, and cleanses you and the deck at the same time.

Grounding can also include prayer. Besides being an age-old connection to a loving source, prayers tend to involve repetition. The censor mind is wholly unimpressed by repetition and may leave the scene out of sheer boredom. Counting very slowly from ten to one yields a similar result.

MY CURRENT FORM OF GROUNDING
IS OPENING MY HEART AND MIND
AS I SAY, "I SERVE THE CREATIVE
UNKNOWN. I SERVE MY INNER CIRCLE.
I SERVE MY OWN CREATIVE DESTINY BY
SERVING THOSE WHO ARE SENT TO ME."

Put your feet firmly on the ground and breathe. Be in your body and in the moment; it will help you open yourself up to vibrancy and life. Distractions and drama give over to spaciousness.

IF READING IN A PUBLIC SPHERE, I
SUGGEST MY CLIENTS IMAGINE THE NOISE
AROUND US AS A LOVELY SOUNDSCAPE FOR
THEIR LIFE.

How will you know when you've finished Grounding? You will feel it; grounding is a sense of entering a different experience of time. It might be experienced as a full stillness, serene and slow. At the very least, it is a haven from loud thoughts and feelings. This time and place of flow is spirit time. Spirit time is a place where the past, present, and future are nonlinear and interchangeable. Grounding draws you fully into the present, creating a completely fluid and accessible past and future.

13

✦

THE SECOND PRINCIPLE: INTENT

The truest question holds the answer

One of the greatest benefits of giving a reading is breaking free from the power of limiting self-narratives. Readings give us different insights that allow new stories and identities to emerge, and show the mythic story at the heart of our lives.

Readings aren't mainly for prediction. Though there will be messages that predict certain events or feelings, many readings raise our level of awareness and the menu of choices in our lives. The power of a true reading is to help your own wisdom, hope, and creativity rise to the occasion. In fact, some readings may aid only in retrospect. They will illustrate a deeper rhythm of life or the Creative Unknown's support in our lives.

If the first Principle of Grounding could be compared to the X on the map that states, "You are here," the second Principle, of Intent, would be your or the seeker's desired destination. The Intent could be a question, request, clarification, or affirmation of the current choices.

Recall that grounding is successfully achieved if one can suspend expected outcomes. Such spaciousness promotes the reading's focus to be about the journey rather than the destination. Trusting the process begins with becoming fully aware of the reason for the reading—the intent.

Reading with Intent means entering a dialogue with spirit rather than reciting an interesting monologue in your head. As in any dialogue, if you're going to ask a question, you need to be open to the answer. Intent, then, is much like pointing your compass north and following the twists and turns that occur along the way.

In looking for an absolute question or intent, know what you know! It may sound obvious, but the obvious is often overlooked. Start by asking a question, and ask what you already know about it. For instance:

"Should I stay in this relationship?"

1. What do I already know?

    I've noticed some red flags in the past six months.

    I've never been good at leaving a relationship until it's well beyond saving.

    Part of me kind of hopes it will fall apart.

    I'm afraid to be alone.

Use your truths to create a clearer focus for the reading. Integrate them into a fuller question so you can find out what you really need to know. The real questions in this particular example might be:

A. Do I have enough faith in myself and/or my partner to face the shortcomings of our relationship?

B. What is needed to be in this relationship fully or leave before it disintegrates further?

C. What is my greatest fear about being alone?

Ask questions that offer choices. Discover what is truly within your ability to change. Real choices come with real power and responsibility. Some questions that might be helpful are:

What is it that I hope to change?

What do I need to know?

What is within my power to affect in this situation?

What insight will give me greater clarity?

What is the message needed at this time?

What am I resisting?

Where is my awareness needed?

Predictive questions such as "yes or no" questions often yield little wisdom. Asking about others' motives or repeating a question in a variety of ways to see if the answer changes are also a disrespectful use of energy. This kind of game playing offers little choice, therefore little responsibility or power.

Asking questions that surrender one's own power leaves one at the mercy of fear. The following are common examples of this "roll the dice" relationship with one's own destiny:

What will happen to me?

Will I ever get married?

What does he think of me?

How long will I live?

Will I win the lottery?

Let's now explore a meditation to discover a more fruitful intent.

The Truest Question

1. Become aware of your breath as you shuffle your full deck face down. Enter spirit time through breathing exercises to clear your mind.

2. Gently shift your focus to all the different questions currently in your life. Let all the unknowns, concerns, and desires flow freely. Don't attach to any one in particular. Keep breathing and let your cards move effortlessly. The question you are looking for may be something that has shown up on your radar recently or perhaps it's been with you

for some time. Is it something you are trying to attempt, or would love to incorporate into your life? Focus on that one core question.

3. Say the question out loud. Do you sense any energy or story released with your verbal expression of it? During this process, you may become aware of fears, influences, and practicalities that may have clouded your truest desire. Finding the heart of your focus is worth your time and the quality of the reading.

4. Explore what you already sense or think you know about this question. Jot your thoughts down if it helps.

5. Now go deeper. What is the feeling or true ache of the question? Is it possible to go deeper? Is there any information you are ignoring or resisting?

6. Once you've surfaced what you really need to know, commit it in writing.

Exploring within for the truest question will start a dialogue with Spirit. The inner and outer connections begin with this intent.

14

The Third Principle: Form

Rituals of the heart yield great insight to life

Intent and Form go together like a hand in a glove. Intent is the question for the reading, and Form is cards chosen in a specific structure; it is the sacred response to intent. In this chapter, we will offer a menu of the cards and spreads. The actual interpreting will be demonstrated in the next chapter, about the principle of synchronicity.

As in Grounding, Form offers another golden opportunity to become the sacred witness. The reader reroutes around ego to making clear choices about the three parts of Form. These are: the initial shuffling or mixing of the cards, determining their direction, and the choice of spread or layout. Although most of the methods described are not necessarily traditional, they will hopefully provide inspiration as well as the mechanics of a reading.

For some readers, mixing the cards means shuffling. Others cut the cards or just hold the deck. Changing the order of the cards in any style allows time during the divination process to focus on the Intent.

It's helpful to allow the cards to move freely. Envision the cards as if they were capable of absorbing all the pros and cons of the intent. These seventy-eight pieces of cardstock showing vivid images, symbols, and stories are transformed as they take up the situation's insecurities or fears. Without fear, we make more creative choices, so finding neutrality at the beginning is a potent action.

As with any of the six principles, mixing cards is an opportunity to open new doors of perception. For instance, if the intent concerns a thorny or emotionally packed issue, a way to acknowledge and release that stuck energy is to mix the cards face down in one big, messy pile. The reader would then choose cards from the chaos.

In your style, shuffle or change the order of the cards until you feel finished. In this "ready" state, you will begin to select the cards for the spread. Choose the cards by impulse rather than overthinking this process. Certain cards will simply feel right to you. They may tingle beneath your fingertips. They may be especially hot or cold. The card needed might be on the very top of the deck or buried deep within its center. The right cards may trigger a light in your mind stating, "This one." There is no wrong way to choose cards. Fanning out all the cards or picking one by one from the deck is perfectly fine. What's important here is mindful choice.

Will you lay the cards face down or face up? This choice may vary from spread to spread or issue to issue. For complicated issues that need a slow, steady pace, consider placing all the cards face down initially. Flip only the cards you are presently focusing on. If the question is fairly straightforward, or you need to see how all the influences are working together, lay all the cards face up when you begin.

When you flip the cards from the deck or in a spread, it helps to turn them over like pages from a book, from left to right. If you flip them up to down, the orientation of the card is changed:

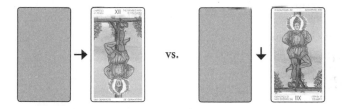

As you can see, flipping the card over up to down can change everything. If you read reversals, upside down cards, preserving the original intent of the card is paramount.

Also consider that many readers opt out of acknowledging reversals and turn all cards upright. Reversals can add a greater variety and deeper insight to a reading, however. Reversed and upright cards are something like the major and minor musical keys. The seventy-eight cards right-side up could be considered the major keys—strong, solid, and stable. The seventy-eight cards upside down could be experienced as the minor keys—slightly mysterious, more subtle, and sometimes haunting. Reversals do not always carry the opposite or negative meaning of the card in its upright position; sometimes it is more of a shift in thinking, or a shade, much like a minor key. For instance, if the Three of Swords came up reversed, it may mean that any pain or the sorrow or grieving is over. Note that this is very different from saying the person is ecstatic or happy. The initial hurt may have passed, but aches may persist, like wounds just beginning to scar. Reversals can capture a subtle tone. Reading a card in its reversed position requires focus, time, and, yes, patience. However, the results could be well worth the cosmic labor. Other insights to reversals could be:

> *The absence of something or someone (if a court card)*
>
> *A hidden issue*
>
> *An area of difficulty*
>
> *Something not quite yet manifested*
>
> *An energy or idea that is out of balance*
>
> *The subject of the card needs more focus than it is currently receiving*

When you shuffle in a way that produces reversals, on rare occasions all the chosen cards are reversed. This could indicate that the information coming through is a completely different perspective for the seeker. In these instances, turn each card upright while keeping in mind that this reading will present new concepts.

How is the orientation of the entire deck determined? How will you know which way is "up" if there are mixed up and down positions? The key may be the bottom card of the deck. This bottom card's direction of being upright or reversed determines the direction of the entire deck. If the way you are holding the deck makes the bottom card appear upside down, turn the deck the opposite direction.

Spreads

It's time to put the selected cards in a spread. A spread can be as small as one card or as large as all seventy-eight! Each spread will either be a form that defines each card's positions, or a spontaneous outline allowing the cards to speak for themselves.

Either way, a helpful boundary for the beginning practitioner is to determine a specific number of cards. Pulling too many cards can be confusing or overstimulating. There is the temptation to keep pulling cards until you get the one you want, rather than the cards you need.

Keep in mind that the actual reading of these spreads will occur in the next chapter. The following information contains designs of various layouts. Experimentation is always encouraged!

The One-Card Spread

There is a lot of power in just one card. A fundamental question such as "What is it I need to know?" can yield tremendous results with a one-card answer. After Grounding and mixing the cards while forming an Intent, select one card. Lay it down face up in front of you.

The Three-Card Spread

Laying three cards can be quite sufficient. The three-card spread can be easily read with defined positions and in a stream-of-consciousness manner. In fact, three cards hold a wealth of possible assignations for the positions (see below).

The three cards can also flow one into the other, unfolding like a story with no designations to the positions. Both ways serve the reader, depending on the intent.

The Path Spread

The Path Spread is an organic flow of three to seven cards. This spread functions well for reading from the beginning to the end, using the cards' imagery to lead you. It is also well suited for any question in which a choice must be made, such as "Should I do this or should I do that?" The Path Spread allows you to explore both. Choose three to seven cards for each path, laying them left to right.

If all time is the present time, then all options are open for exploration. Gaining insight into each option will help the seeker be proactive. Let's say you're looking for a new job, and you have two possible positions open to you. Rather than choosing blindly, gain insight into both. The different paths outline the likely ways each choice would be experienced.

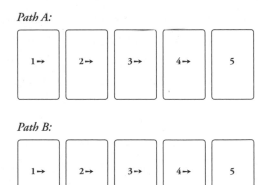

Path A:

| 1→ | 2→ | 3→ | 4→ | 5 |

Path B:

| 1→ | 2→ | 3→ | 4→ | 5 |

A variation of the Path Spread is to initially pick one card signifying the question's very essence. Choose this card unconsciously, keeping it face down. The five placed in a row underneath this essence card are the perspectives or influences needed for greater understanding. This act of clarifying the focus of the question itself allows for a more thorough response.

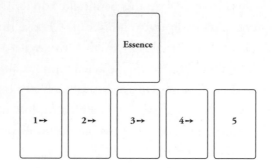

The Celtic Cross Spread

The Celtic Cross is by far the most well-known tarot spread. This isn't surprising, as Arthur Waite created it for his ubiquitous deck. Like a classic theme, it has many variations. We will offer a traditional and modern version.

The Celtic Cross is usually comprised of ten to eleven cards. Each position denotes the card's significance. It is a very useful structure to focus on a multi-faceted or complicated issue. The spread brims with detailed information.

A Traditional Celtic Spread

As adapted from *Simple Fortunetelling with Tarot Cards: Corrine Kenner's Complete Guide.*

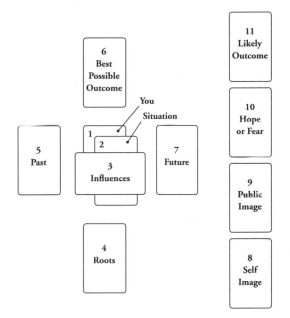

1. **Significator**—You or the seeker

2. **Covering Card**—The situation

3. **Crossing Card**—The energy of the moment and the forces affecting the situation

4. **Foundation Card**—This is the foundation of the situation

5. **Recent Past**—The last six months to a year

6. **Crowning Card**—The best possible outcome of the current situation

7. **Near Future**—The next six months to a year

8. **Self Image**—How you see yourself, or the seeker sees him- or herself

9. **Public Image**—How others see you or the seeker

10. **Hopes and Fears**—Any hopes and fears—the dreams one almost doesn't dare to dream

11. **Most Likely Outcome**—The most likely outcome of your or the seeker's current path

A Modern Celtic Spread—The Wellsian Celtic

The Wellsian Spread is adapted from an original spread by James Wells, a Toronto-based tarot consultant, circle host, and reiki teacher who can be found at http://jameswells .wordpress.com.

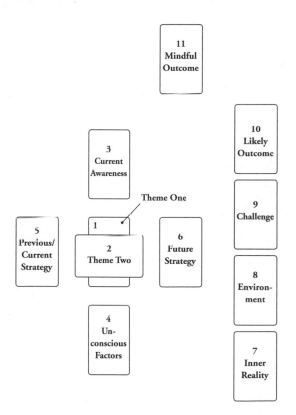

1. **First Core Rhythm**—A theme in the seeker's life right now

2. **Second Core Rhythm**—A second theme in the seeker's life right now

All the other cards enhance these two core cards which represent the seeker's energies.

3. **Conscious Factors**—The seeker's current awareness of cards 1 and 2

4. **Unconscious Factors**—Unknown or subtle factors surrounding this situation

5. **Previous Strategy**—A strategy the seeker has used before, but is something the seeker is leaving behind or should leave behind

6. **Future Strategy**—A strategy or new focus the seeker should move toward

7. **Inner Reality**—The seeker's true situation

8. **Outer Reality**—All that is not the seeker in this situation, the outside environment

9. **The Challenge**—The opportunity or obstacle to be learned at this time

10. **Most Likely Outcome**—What will likely happen as a result of the core rhythms according to the seeker's current choices and awareness

11. **Mindful Outcome**—What would the situation look like with the willingness to change reactive thoughts or feelings?

The Circle Spread

A beautiful, organic spread can simply be a circle. The card in the middle represents the seeker or the question. The three to seven cards surrounding it are the various influences or perspectives to consider.

Again, as in any spread, a card can act as a free agent or is defined by its position in the spread. The exception is any card representing the seeker and/or the significator, which always represents the seeker.

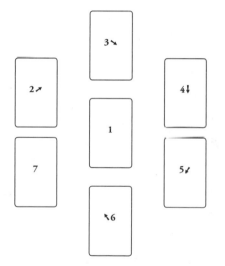

As with any aspect of intuition, creativity opens many new doors. Here are a few ideas of how to create your own spreads.

Design a spread as if diagramming a sentence. For instance, the central person would be the noun in the question. The verb would be the action wanted or needed.

Each component would have its own card. For those who love language, this could be a compelling structure.

What would the design of the spread look like if it contained or symbolized the energy of the question? For example, if the issue calls to mind the effort needed to climb a mountain, design the layout in the outline of a mountain with a specific number of cards. The card representing the seeker could "climb" each position until he or she reaches the summit. The sky truly is the limit when it comes to designing and using spreads.

Now that you've Grounded, created an Intent, and learned about Form, you must be itching to read the cards. In the next chapter, about Synchronicity, you will.

15

THE FOURTH PRINCIPLE: SYNCHRONICITY

The truth is always revealed to those who are ready

Synchronicity is the sacred response to the question or request of a reading. The idea of Synchronicity is that simultaneous events are meaningfully related. Jung coined the word to describe the governing dynamic that underlies the whole human experience on all levels. Readings encompass synchronicity in their shuffling, the selection of certain cards, and each card's particular viewpoint. Synchronicity is the flow, and the reading is trusting in the flow, no matter what.

O NE OF MY FAVORITE DEFINITIONS OF SYNCHRONICITY IS "THE DIVINE GIGGLE."

The polar opposite of this flow is "luck," a paradigm that promotes separateness and powerlessness. As a prime example, many readers (and sometimes seekers) will question if the cards selected are actually the correct ones— were the wrong ones chosen by mistake? The cards in question are often distressing or dark-looking ones. Luck is the underlying current of these kinds of doubt and does not determine any step of the reading process. In fact, if the two major forces at work in any reading are love and fear, then luck is the middle child of fear. There are no "wrong" cards.

I TELL CLIENTS THAT IF THEY INDEED
SELECTED THE "WRONG CARD," ITS IMAGE
WILL CHANGE BEFORE IT IS TURNED
FACE UP.

Another interference with the flow of Synchronicity is the need to be consistent. Our culture values a consistent train of thought and a consistent message with no ambiguity or loose ends. Unfortunately, clinging to validation through consistency can cause one to bypass valuable information. In the beginning, observe all and exclude nothing.

From the first moment of Grounding to the last moment of Closure, everything that happens is synchronistic and part of the reading. Grounding allows a reader to gain

entrance into the web of time—past, present, and future—
where all is possible. In this space, it's as if all worlds of reality converge. Even environmental sounds such as a bark-
ing dog, a faraway train whistle, an ambulance siren, or a
phone call during this sacred time may contribute greatly
to the reading.

I SUGGEST MY CLIENTS NOTE WHO PHONED
DURING THE READING. THE CALLER OR
THE MESSAGE MIGHT SHED LIGHT ON THE
CLIENT'S READING. EVEN THE TIMING OF A
PESKY SALES CALL SPEAKS VOLUMES ABOUT
THE QUESTION WE WERE INVESTIGATING.

A common synchronistic event is a card flying or falling
out of the pack. Those errant cards are very important—
they're literally flying to get your attention! If you choose
not to use them exclusively as the Divine response, at least
incorporate their contribution into the overall message.

*I was never more aware of synchronicity than when I
was reading at a party several years ago. I'd found a
private corner to read downstairs. The hostess and her
friends came down one at a time for a reading.*

*One of the younger women came downstairs.
She was rather timid, and as the reading went on, I
discovered she had a bully of a husband. I began to*

counsel her about the importance of standing up for herself.

I had not even finished the thought when the hostess's son stormed into the room, full of righteous rage over a tarot reader being in his house. At first, I asked him to please wait, and I would address his complaints when I had finished with the reading. When that didn't work, I realized that now might be an opportunity the universe was offering. I leaned over to the young woman I was reading for and said, "I think I'm about to give you an example of how to defend yourself."

I held my ground firmly through his bluster of name-calling and ridicule. When he paused for a breath, I recommended he bring the situation to his mother, who had invited me into their home. He stomped out of the room, and out of the house. I then tended to my frightened client, reassuring her that courage is an act of love.

Hopefully your encounters with Synchronicity will not be nearly as explosive, but they will be just as meaningful. Let's start this exploration with the exercises below.

The One-Card Reading

Holding your deck, close your eyes and acknowledge all the ways your focus and efforts have been at work recently. Honor those efforts and let them slowly fade away until you can feel your "creative eyes," eyes that see clearly the mystery of life. Focus on one question or issue and pick one card. Lay the card face down in front of you.

Before flipping the card over from left to right, sense the card's energy and decide if you'll read it as a reversal. Acknowledge and release any initial judgment of the image, especially the knee-jerk reaction of "good" or "bad." Look at the image as the Divine response to your question. Based on your question, does it make sense at all? When you flipped the card over, what did it trigger?

Go deeper. Let the story of this image speak to you. Is it a reflection of you or your life? What connections does it elicit? What is the message coming from your great loving source?

Don't dismiss any out-of-the-blue feelings or thoughts. Know that rational responses aren't necessarily true ones. Trust what you see with your heart, and be open to the information that comes at you sideways—those quick flashes are rare and valuable.

Write down your impressions, especially the ones that don't make sense. You'll be surprised at the bigger picture that begins to form over the next forty-eight hours.

For those who don't feel comfortable swan-diving into a card, try a layered approach. There are three styles in viewing a card: literal, symbolic, and psychic. Each style can be used exclusively or as a layer for the other two—psychic builds on symbolic, which builds on literal. Let's explore these layers in one card and then with the Circle spread.

One-Card Reading

Literal Viewing: The title is Death. A skeletal warrior is riding on a white horse. He carries a banner in his right hand. The banner shows one white flower design. A royal figure seems dead from being trampled. A bishop figure seems to be pleading or saying something to Death. To the right is a bright sunset between two pillars in the distance. There is also a waterfall and a boat.

Symbolic Viewing: The skeleton is a proud warrior. The bones of the matter are undeniable. Black and white colors dominate the picture. There isn't much gray when it comes to dying. The sun setting behind the two pillars may be symbolic of the end of the day or death being part of a natural cycle. The pillars are a gateway to another world. The five-petal rose is a symbol of life. The river with the boat in the background is reminiscent of the River Styx, on which Charon ferries souls to the underworld. Death bears the number thirteen on his flag, a mysterious number. The king pictured is dead—Death is more powerful than all the riches and prestige in the world.

Psychic Viewing: The end is bringing the new form. I feel the glow of the sun, yet its warmth will soon be gone. Nothing can stop this cycle of death and birth. I feel as if I am the young girl in the corner of the card. I really don't want to pay attention to the changes in my life. I'm kind of hoping my faith will be able to smooth over the bad stuff. What would have happened if I paid attention? Change is inevitable—what if I was a willing participant? How could I affect others if I was paying attention, but was also accepting of life's realities?

The Circle Spread

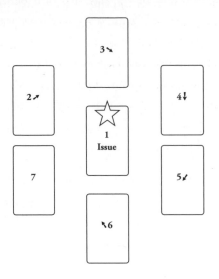

Focus on one specific issue, relationship, or facet of your life. Draw one card to represent you, and lay it face up as card 1. Place three to six cards in a circle face up around the middle card. Designate a card in the circle as the first card. Read the remaining cards in the circle in a clockwise direction starting with card 2 and relating each card to the center card. Allow for time while using a soft gaze.

Think of the cards as containing levels of information. The first level is literal. What do you actually see? It might be a bird, a wheel, or three women. Name all the different symbols and characters that catch your eye or seem important or charged. Is there a common visual element, like a color, object, animal, or land feature? Write down all the things in each card that stand out. See a story start to form from the similarities.

Next, look at the cards symbolically. Do any symbols, such as the female symbol in the Empress card or the crosses in the Hierophant card, stir up any feelings or sensations? Things become symbols when given meaning. Reading the cards symbolically means looking for those elements and images that invoke personal meaning. Pay particular attention to the parts within each card that feel charged. Not every single symbol is necessary or requires your attention; you're looking for symbols that are very alive or elicit a deep, internal response. What are those responses?

Finally, look at each card psychically, with Sight—with soft eyes and an open heart. If you were to describe all these cards in relation to you as the central figure, what new truths or ideas come to you? What movie or images appear on your mind's silver screen? These stories don't need to be related directly to information gleaned from a card. Some of the stories may fly in sideways. What secrets do these cards hold for you? Are there things you don't want to see or hear? Are you purposely ignoring something?

A three- to six-card spread can take some time and practice to read. Trust your storytelling skills and let your imagination run free.

Using a variation of the Wellsian Celtic Spread, we'll explore how the card is also defined by its position in the spread.

A Wellsian Celtic Spread Variation

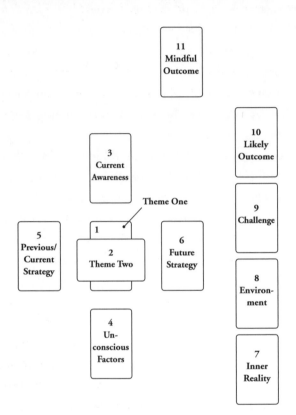

Shuffle the cards and focus on your entire current life as if it were a movie. What has been on your radar lately? Have there been greater issues? Do you notice any major themes? What about concerns or desires? As you shuffle, let all the ways life is dancing with you go into the cards.

When you feel ready, follow the diagram and lay the cards face down.

Put the rest of the deck aside. Flipping left to right, turn over cards 1 and 2. According to the Creative Unknown (or your version of a greater source/love), these two cards have been specifically selected to display the two core rhythms of your life. How would you describe them? Do you recognize these rhythms? Rather than describing the image itself, describe what it triggers for you, rational or not.

According to your Divine committee, what purpose is there in becoming acutely aware of these two energies? Look at their relationship to each other. Is there a flow? Is there tension? If so, do you sense a timeline of this particular dynamic? Is this an age-old pattern or a new experience? Do you agree with what these core cards are revealing? For instance, would you consider these two rhythms to be the most profound ones in your life now?

Now move on to cards 3 and 4. Card 3 represents your awareness of this interplay. Since this position represents consciousness, the information is probably not surprising. The card itself may be surprising, but by its position, you are aware of its message on some level.

Card 4 holds information of which you are unaware. Look closely at the card. Can you sense what it is trying to tell you? Do you know what the information might be? Might it be something you are underestimating or overlooking? If it's a court card, can you think of someone who serves as a major influence, but behind the scenes? Alternatively, is this someone whose approval you unknowingly seek? Since this card represents an unknown, the information may simply remain subtle or hidden at first glance. Record your impressions, keeping in mind that first impressions carry a lot of weight.

Next is card 5. This card represents a strategy you are outgrowing as related to the two rhythms. Does this card illustrate what you've been doing? Does card 5 show a new perspective on this strategy?

Turn over card 6. It informs you of which new ways of focus and effort are helpful. How could the two core energies move in a nourishing way? How could this particular new shift in focus benefit you directly? What do you think card 6's message is? Let any received information fill you completely. Rather than trying to grab for answers, let them walk up to you.

Card 7 reveals your deepest reality about your relationship with life itself. How do you feel about your life right now? Keep in mind this card might depict a more honest picture than you are willing to admit. Take in the answer without judging it. You can disagree with it later, but accept the information at least briefly before disregarding it.

Now turn over card 8. This position determines an outer reality. This might be how others would see the current expression of your two major dynamics. It could also indicate the things which are simply beyond your power, such as timing, the environment, the cosmic flow, or other people. What does this card say to you?

Card 9 reveals the challenge or the gift of your core issues. It reflects the struggle or the benefit of being in your life fully. If these two major themes were integrated well, how would that affect everyday living?

The possible outcome of the situation is reflected in card 10. If the two rhythms progress in their present state without any shift of thought, attitude, or action, card 10 shows the most likely result. What does card 10 tell you about the outcome you are heading toward?

Even if card 10 displays a desired outcome, pick an eleventh card. Card 11 will present an image that would occur if there were additional mindfulness. It becomes the representation of the authentic result, the one that is most nourishing to you, not necessarily the desired one.

A Traditional Celtic Sample Reading

Imagine a man has come to you for a reading. His role will be denoted by an "S" for Seeker. Your role will be indicated by "R" for Reader.

R: I'm glad you've come in for a reading. What would you like to explore today?

S: I've been wondering if I should go back to school, or stay in my current job.

R: What would you say is your current leaning?

S: (*Shrugs*) There's good and bad in both, I guess.

R: So you're not sure.

S: Well, I feel like I've gone as far as I can go at my job. It's starting to get boring, and I don't feel like

I'm learning much. But they appreciate me there and I'm good at it. On the other hand, if I go back to school ... I mean, I've got three payments left on my student loans. It's just, it's a big commitment of time and money, and I'm not sure it's the right choice. I'm wondering if I should pursue some of the other things I was interested in before this job.

R: All right then. We'll see if we can't shed some more light on this decision today. Would you mind choosing any one of these decks?

The seeker chooses a deck. As you look through the cards, you hold an image of the Seeker's appearance and his current situation. When you see the Page of Rods, it feels like "Bingo!" You choose that card as the significator. You lay it down between you.

R: I'm hearing that you may not feel like you are progressing unless you are learning. If it's all right with you, I would like to explore not only the needed insights for your very big lifestyle decision, but also more about the message regarding learning, no matter what you should decide. Please close your eyes and shuffle the cards. Let go of all of your attached outcomes. As you do that, I'm going to close my eyes and go in a little deeper.

You close your eyes and drift into your center. From there, you branch out your psychic sense to find an initial im-

age of the seeker in his situation. In your mind, you see a knight returning home from the Crusades. The war is over, and he is idle and bored. The deeper question that surfaces is "How do you maintain when the war is over? How does one make do in times of peace?" You hold this image of the tired, restless knight as you open your eyes.

R: Just hand me the deck whenever you feel finished with shuffling, when the deck feels right. I'm going to lay a Celtic Spread to see if we can't fully explore the issue before us.

You lay the Traditional Celtic spread. Every card is face down except for the Significator.

R: We'll turn these over as we get to them so we can focus on one aspect at a time.

For reference: "R" indicates a reversal

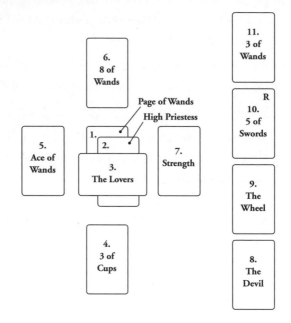

R: (*Flips over the High Priestess and the Lovers*) It looks like you're going to need to approach this situation with wisdom. Are you in a relationship right now?

S: (*Surprised*) Yes, how did you know?

R: It looks like your relationship may be a factor to consider in this decision. Is this serious? Are you planning to get married?

S: (*Blushes*) Um... well, we haven't talked about it yet. We've been going out a few months.

R: It looks like this is or could become a very significant relationship for you. How would returning to
school affect this relationship if it did turn into a
deep commitment?

S: Well, if I went back to school, it'd be hard to find
time to be together. The school is a two-hour com-
mute away.

R: That's something to consider. You are at a major
crossroads right now. I can tell from just these two
cards that this decision could be a turning point in
your life. It's not only a decision about work and
school, but the potential relationship of a lifetime
is at stake.

S: Okay. Wow.

R: Let's see what you have for a foundation card (*flips
the Three of Cups*). It looks like you've had a lot of
success in your past. And possibly a few partners as
well?

S: Um … well, yeah. I've had a few relationships but
nothing really serious. I mean there were always all
these other things to get done, you know? That next
hurdle. This is the most serious I've ever been, with
Kim.

R: So would you say this is the first time you haven't
been sure what that next hurdle is?

S: Yeah, that's exactly it. I finished high school. Went
to college. Finished college. Went hunting for that

cherry job, and eventually I got that, too. I guess I just never thought about what happens after that.

R: (*Flips over the Ace of Wands*) You've been in your current job for at least a year.

S: Two years.

R: You really fit in there.

S: Yeah, I do.

R: (*Flips over the Eight of Wands*) I see the potential for some fast growth. Whatever decision you make, the outcome is going to come quickly. Let's look at the next six months. (*Flips over Strength—For some reason, the card triggers ideas of leadership and a person who can manage power well. This style of leadership is extremely valuable*). Yeah, I definitely wouldn't count your current job out yet. It looks like you'd be really happy with where it goes. I think you're about to be offered a leadership position.

S: Really? I mean, I can see that. I just ... I never really saw myself in a leadership role. I've always preferred to keep learning.

R: Well, this leadership position isn't a death sentence. It looks as though both school and job will be opportunities for learning. In fact, if you did go back to school, you'd want to look into management training or something else that will get you into a leadership role. I think you have some rare, untapped abilities in that area.

S: Huh. I suppose I won't know until I try it.

R: Just give it some thought. (*Flips the Devil*) Hmm. You really do hate inertia, don't you.

S: I get a little restless, yeah.

R: What I'm getting is that you feel trapped because you don't feel like you're moving.

S: (*Laughs*) Yeah, I'm not a stand-still kind of guy.

R: (*Flips the Wheel of Fortune*) Wow, this is a big decision. When we're done here, I'm really going to encourage you to think long and well. Make a list of priorities. You don't want to make a decision just to feel any kind of movement. This decision and commitment to any three of these subjects could set the foundation for the rest of your life.

S: I'm starting to get that picture myself.

R: Good. As for the Wheel here, you might see yourself as trapped. But others are really seeing you as growing up.

You get a flash of the Crusade knight again charging onto the scene. "Where is the king? I need the king to tell me what to do!" he says.

S: Yeah?

R: Yes. In fact, when you first came in here, I got this image of you as knight returning from the Crusades. You seemed bored. There is no adventure in maintaining the kingdom. Knights are all about orders and action, not vision or design. I think I'm seeing a deeper issue here.

S: A deeper issue?

R: Others see you growing into your power. You're not the knight anymore. You don't need a king to tell you what to do. You're reaching a transitional point in your life. You're a king in training. Does that make sense?

S: Yeah, in a weird way.

R: Let's see what fears are getting in the way of the situation here (*flips over the Five of Swords reversed*). Yes, you're heading to a part of life where the learning will be inner movement, rather than outer movement. You are new to this kind of adventure. It's going to feel odd to do the shift, but that is where your true power resides, waiting.

S: "Odd" is putting it mildly.

R: (*Flips over the Three of Wands*) I think what you want to do at this point is really take a good look at your horizons. If you really hate inertia so much, if you really can't stand it, an easy way out is to go ahead and go back to school. That will most certainly cause chaos in your relationship and with your finances.

S: (*Laughs*) Yeah, no doubt.

R: But this might be a situation where stillness is needed. Let's pull a final clarity card on that.

S: Okay.

R: Now, I want you to close your eyes. Imagine yourself as an old man. You've lived a long, full life, and you've grown in wisdom and experience. You have completely manifested your destiny. I want you to ask the older version of yourself what insight he might have for you in regard to your current situation.

You fan out the rest of the deck and extend it toward him.

R: Choose a card you feel holds the energy of his answer. Don't think too hard about it. Which card feels right?

S: (*Chooses a card and hands it to you*) This one.

R: (*Flips over the Five of Wands and lays it with the rest of the spread*) Yes. You definitely cannot make this choice based on comfort. Discomfort is necessary for change at times, like this one. Consider there are all kinds of movement, all kinds of learning.

S: So, inertia.

R: Yeah, inertia.

S: Great.

R: (*Smiles*) Don't lose heart. Transform that inertia into the time and space to make a very clear choice. Your quality of life may well depend on your ability to do just this. It shouldn't be rushed or made out of restlessness.

S: So, what now?

R: Well, for the time being, give yourself forty-eight hours with the information we've gathered here today. Don't make any big decisions. Just let the reading simmer in the back of your head. You should also pay attention to your dreams or signs during this time. You might get some more insights.

S: Okay.

R: And I'd recommend you speak to the fearless knight within to see what he needs to be a content king. Call for another reading if you're still restless in a couple of seasons.

S: Sounds good.

R: Thank you so much for coming in today.

S: Yeah, thank you. We'll definitely be in touch.

R: I would love to hear how it goes.

All versions of the Celtic Cross are helpful for those who don't feel comfortable moving about the cards by intuition alone. If you feel the need for less structure, however, try a reading that flows like storytelling. The classic story structure of exposition, climax, and resolution can be used to form a powerful spread. To illustrate, we will use the accessible Path Spread.

The Path Spread

Path A:

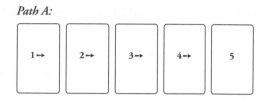

Path B:

Think of an area or decision needing clarification. Work, health, or relationships are often major contenders! For the purpose of this exercise, select an issue that presents two different possibilities or choices. For instance, "Should I stay in Minneapolis or move to Seattle?" Focus on both of the choices as you blend the cards.

When you're finished shuffling, focus on Path A. Pick three to five cards that seem to contain the energy for this decision. Lay them face up, left to right.

Repeat this for your second choice, Path B.

After both paths have cards, return to Path A to focus on its cards for a few minutes. How would you describe the experience if you made this choice? Try to recognize it as a story from beginning to end. How does this path play out? How does it progress? What is the central theme? If you were the main character in each of the cards, what would be your reality of Path A? Does this path hold a satisfying outcome for you? Did you expect this outcome? Note any significant impressions in your journal.

Now study and translate Path B in the same manner.

Other questions that might provide insight for the storytelling style are:

- Is there a particular suit that keeps showing up? If so, what does that element represent to you currently?

- Are there many court cards? What might the cards be saying about the people who will be involved in this path? Which parts of your personality might be most stimulated/starved by this decision?

- Can you see patterns pointing to a certain message?

Rather than showing yes or no answers or putting runway lights on a particular path, the Path spread encourages you to delve into the experience of both decisions. The pattern of laying the cards from left to right naturally encourages a story to develop.

A Path Spread Variation

Imagine a young woman has come to you for a reading. Her role will be denoted by "S" for Seeker. Your role will be denoted by "R" for Reader. You are sitting side by side, rather than facing each other. Five decks are in front of the seeker, face up.

R: Well the very first thing I'll ask of you is to go shopping. I would like you to pick just one of these five decks. Look at some more of the images if you need to. Pick the style of art that you prefer (*the seeker chooses a deck*).

R: What brought you to a reading today? What could use some different insight right now?

S: I'm worried about this new guy I'm dating. I'm not sure how the relationship's going to go.

R: Great, let's begin. We are going to let go of the world during this reading. Please put your fingertips on the deck. Close your eyes for a moment and let all the pros and cons of this relationship, of life, of everything slowly dissipate with each breath. You might feel an opening within to just be yourself.

During the Grounding, you ask to receive an initial image. You receive no image, simply a message that it's all in the cards.

R: Now, I want you to shuffle the deck, thinking about your relationship. Let all your hopes and fears about it flow through your fingertips right into the cards, as if they were big sponges. Shuffle the deck until it feels right to you. At that point, one card is going to call to you. It will feel hot or cold; it may tingle. Somehow, this card will make itself known to you. Take as long as you need.

The seeker shuffles and eventually pulls the Seven of Wands. You take the deck back from the Seeker, checking the bottom card to make sure the deck is properly oriented. You then proceed to lay five more cards beneath the Seven of Wands in the Path spread variation.

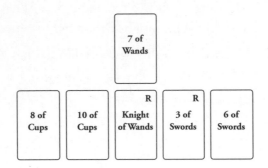

("R" indicates a Reversal)

R: The first card chosen is the Seven of Wands. It would indicate that you're feeling a bit guarded about your new relationship, is that true? *(As a reader, you notice a movement of growth and joy through the Eight of Cups and the Ten of Cups. However, that energy stalls upon reaching the Knight of Wands and the Three of Swords, by someone who is no longer present and by old pain. The flow will return.)*

S: Yes, I suppose so.

R: *(Indicating the Knight of Wands)* There was someone before. You'd really pinned your hopes on him.

S: *(Surprised)* Well … yes.

R: (*Indicating the Eight of Cups*) I see the new guy is still somewhat of a mystery to you. You haven't allowed your heart to see deep into his heart because this old relationship is still standing in your way. This man (*indicating the Knight of Wands*) left you completely burned, didn't he?

S: (*Tears up a little*) I thought he was the one, you know? I thought we were going to have a family together, build a life.

R: (*Hands her a tissue and gives her some time*) I can see you were unhappy to see the relationship end (*indicates the Three of Swords*). I think you're still hanging on to some of that. You're not quite at peace with the old relationship being over. But it's over, and it is standing in the way of this new relationship, which shows all the promise of being a good, worthwhile relationship (*indicates the Ten of Cups*).

You note the lack of pentacles and the major arcana. You see that the wands in the spread are right on top of each other.

R: I can see that you feel unprotected. The boundaries are weak, so you are over-vigilant in defending yourself from men like him (*indicates the Knight of Wands*). This new guy doesn't have the secret password for your trust (*indicates the Seven of Wands*). He is, however, a deeply emotional person, nothing like your old boyfriend who disappointed you so badly. Can you see that?

S: Yeah, I guess I do see that. I can talk to Max more openly already.

R: (*Indicates the Ten of Cups*) Max makes you feel great, doesn't he?

S: Actually, yes. Yes he does. It's just ... really hard to trust that feeling.

R: Trust is the only way to move forward (*indicates the Six of Swords*). You need to give the guy a chance. You want to be moving forward in your life.

S: Definitely.

R: I'm going to pull a final clarity card to know what might help you move ahead without fear.

S: Okay.

You pull the Four of Wands.

R: Hmmm. Let me ask you something. In your last relationship, did you have all your hopes and dreams attached to that man?

S: Well, yes. I really wanted a family, and I thought we were going to have this great life, you know?

R: Before you go any further in the relationship with Max or any significant relationship, you need to decide what you want from your love affair with life. What would make you happy about your life if you were all by yourself? You need to have the vision before building the foundation. If you decide to take a partner for the journey, so be it.

S: I...I guess so. That's not the first time I got that message. I just figured I could get around it, darn it!

R: Just think about it. Don't make any decisions for the next twenty-four hours. Just let the reading simmer in the back of your mind for a while. It might bring up some new things for you to consider.

S: Okay.

R: Pay attention to your dreams, too. Your own wisdom may be triggered and have way more important things to say than I ever could!

S: Okay.

R: I'm afraid we need to be done for today, but we can do another reading in a few weeks or so if you want. How are you feeling?

S: Like I have a lot to think about.

R: I've really enjoyed reading for you today. Be good to yourself.

S: I'll try... thanks!

Trust the synchronicity of your story. If you receive cards that don't make any sense or fail to elicit any response, trust *that* as the answer. Tell yourself, "This card tells me I'm confused." Or perhaps you are not meant to know the answer at this time.

TAROT IS FULL OF MOMENTS THAT FEEL
AS THOUGH THE DIVINE HAS A SENSE
OF HUMOR. IT DOES, AND IT HELPS.

❧

Learning to read is a process of getting comfortable with uncertainty. Get used to the way energy dances with you. Relax as you learn how to dance backwards!

16

The Fifth Principle: Closure

We deeply bow to those who brighten our inner light

Closure is a profound yet often overlooked part of sacred communication and is essential after venturing into other worlds and dimensions. Our bodies and gravity demand a different existence than spirit time, where all things converge. If we don't perform some act of closure, we risk becoming scattered, confused, or irritable for the rest of the day or longer. It's important for our bodies, minds, and spirits to return to linear time smoothly.

Performing an act of closure is much like saying goodbye to good friends. You thank all those who were there, feel gratitude, and then have a ritual of departure or goodbye.

A steadfast ritual with tarot is to choose one last card. This final card is the reading's last thought or idea. After turning it over and reading it, you can blow out the candles, smudge the space, or ring a bell with mindfulness to close the last veil to the sanctuary between worlds. Simply reshuffling all the cards with eyes closed in gratitude for the information received is also effective. When you return to "human" time, you should feel relaxed, even if the issues were tough.

I SUGGEST MY CLIENTS REFRAIN FROM MAKING ANY DECISIONS ABOUT THE READING RIGHT AWAY. INSTEAD, THEY SHOULD LET THE DUST SETTLE OVER THE NEXT FORTY-EIGHT HOURS, TO SEE WHAT NEW CONNECTIONS HAVE BEEN MADE.

If you still experience disorientation, anxiety, or depletion after Closure, it's not that you did it incorrectly. There may have been insufficient grounding in the first place, or you may have read for too long. In the beginning, consider keeping a reading to thirty minutes at most. As you close your readings, be sure to thank any spirits that showed (including your own), and be sure you close the curtains on Spirit time.

17

The Sixth Principle: Integration

Choices made in love bear fruit

Integrating the wisdom gained from a reading is the biggest challenge of divination. Unless absorbed, the knowledge slips away. It's as if the information from between the worlds wants to return there, and it certainly will if the seeker does not heed its wisdom. The information that has been gathered is meant to act as a catalyst for your own wisdom. If you do not integrate what you felt and sensed was true direction, a sacred amnesia takes over. Actually, sacred amnesia is desirable when reading others! You are not meant to hold knowledge for another—it is for the seeker alone. When gleaning information for yourself, however, enact the new shifts that will better your life path.

By its nature, the sixth principle is the most challenging because it requires change. Most of us are allergic to change. It requires breaking patterns and forming new habits. Incorporating even just one new idea is a good start.

I TELL CLIENTS I WON'T SAY ANYTHING THEY DON'T ALREADY KNOW. IT'S JUST WEIRD WHEN A COMPLETE STRANGER SAYS IT ALOUD.

In truth, you may begin to lose some of the insights you were given almost as soon as the reading is over. Shortly after a reading, capture the essence of what initially rang true for you. First impressions are always important. What surprised you? Might you feel, think, or act differently with these new perspectives?

Let the reading linger for the next forty-eight hours. Do not make any life decisions based on the reading during this time. There may be unconscious shifts, so pay attention to dreams, new ideas, surplus energy, or new ways of perceiving life.

After the forty-eight-hour incubation period, see if there is still one truth that "sparkles" on its own. Is there one action you could commit to based on this wisdom? What one truth is ready to surface on a more conscious level? How might you incorporate this sacred information to nourish your life?

I once read for a twenty-one-year-old woman who was very distressed. After I served her a cup of tea, we grounded with each other and proceeded to do an hour-long reading.

It wasn't long before I found myself amazed. As her life unfolded before me, I saw it as though I were looking at myself at twenty-one. If I had gone to an accurate reader when I was twenty-one years old, my reading would have been this one!

The core message of the reading was a clear warning that her life would come tumbling down within the next year due to a fairly destructive relationship and many unresolved past issues. Unless she could learn to meet those challenges head-on and in a different manner, her house of cards would fall down around her. The reading gave specific actions and shifts that would prevent inevitable pain.

She seemed rather shocked, yet on some level knew these truths. These were the same messages her heart had been trying to get to her for some time. I gave her information honestly and openly. I wasn't sure if she would make the changes or not.

Three years after this electric reading, the young woman booked another appointment. As we proceeded to start a new reading, she told me that indeed all the predictions had come to pass. She said she wished she'd heeded that advice. She was now starting from zero and pulling the pieces back together.

I realized I would have made the same choices at twenty-one years old, even with the reading. Even though you may receive the exact map you need, you still may not be ready to act on its wisdom in your life.

We are given information at the exact time we need it most. But without change, that knowledge cannot take root in our lives—it dissipates like smoke.

18

READING TAROT WITH THE SIGHT

The dance of all of your gifts is destiny

Sight and tarot skills have been treated separately up to this point. In this chapter, we'll recap the six principles before demonstrating the various combinations of tarot and psychic readings. The examples are designed for the reader-seeker relationship, but are easily adapted for solo readings if preferred.

A Brief Summary

What concepts have led us to this point? First and foremost, everything is composed of and connected by energy. One reads energy by using one's heightened intuitive sense, referred to as Sight. This "channel" requires a different usage of the senses and time.

We have also explored tarot's structure. This system of seventy-eight cards provides a rich, visual language. Its imagery invites exploration into the human experience through stories.

Both Sight and the tarot require a willingness to shift from the linear, productive everyday thinking to the observer's timeless curiosity. This timelessness is often experienced as a spaciousness of uninterrupted flow allowing one's heart, mind, and spirit to move freely. Connected to a larger source of love, one is free from habitual or projected ways of experiencing realities.

The reading itself is an act of seeing the ordinary as extraordinary. The past, present, or future life may be explored with new potential and choice. This viewing creates the possibility of living and loving one's life fully.

An accessible structure for any form of divination is the six principles, which are:

1. **Grounding**—Begin by entering the spiritual realm by becoming fully present through measured breathing and an inward focus.

2. **Intent**—Seek the truest need or focus for this reading through clear introspection of motives and prioritization.

3. **Form**—Choose the cards and spreads for the reading.

4. **Synchronicity**—Gather all energetic messages, insights, ideas, and patterns.

5. **Closure**—Gather all the cards and give thanks.

6. **Integration**—After a brief time for further contemplation, decide how to bring the relevant insights into everyday life.

You may want to review any concepts listed here that remain unclear at this point. Repetition and absorption of the ideas and exercises will further your confidence in expressing your intuitive abilities.

Psychic Tarot

The initial image or snapshot of the seeker's current reality sets the reading into motion. The tarot's images, along with the seeker's truths and any accompanying loving, invisible beings all move together, like dancers. None are more important than the other. The six principles serve as the structure for a grounded experience for both reader and seeker. The reader is responsible for the reading's flow of information, pace, and intensity.

Let's look at the spectrum of readings from solely tarot to psychic channeling. You will undoubtedly feel more comfortable with one or two styles. Experimenting with each kind of reading will give you more choices for your readings. In the following examples, the seeker is a woman receiving a reading for the first time.

1. *A Tarot Reading*

Grounding: Have the seeker select a deck by choosing her favorite artistic style. Tell her to hold the deck. Suggest that she go within herself and picture her life swirling around her, but not within her. Offer her gentle guidance: "Let all the pros and cons of your life spiral around you as you enjoy the neutral center." Explain that she should feel free to speak during the reading, especially if she is confused or disagrees with anything.

Intent: Ask some initial questions to find the Intent for the reading, such as: "What brings you to a reading?" or "Which areas could use different insight?" Echo her responses and encourage any clarification to find the core questions. Have her shuffle the deck and pull two cards, face down.

Form: The big picture can be captured in an overview spread. This six-card spread is a simple yet profound introduction of the seeker's current life lessons and her responses to them. Cards 1 and 2 are the heart themes for the seeker. Card 3 represents her head—the awareness of these two themes. Card 4 is her left hand, what she is capable of receiving from the universe currently. Card 5 is her right hand, what she is manifesting. The last card is card 6, which represents the next step. Lay this spread in the form of a body with cards 1 and 2 in the center. After you have a strong direction from the overview spread, use three to six cards in the Path spread or any variation as responses for the topics and questions that arise throughout the remainder of the session.

Synchronicity: Share all relevant triggers from the cards. Let the cards speak to you through their symbols and stories. Take the time to ponder as you find the images that seem charged and vital. Encourage the seeker to share her triggers and reactions as well. Remain aware of her responses to the cards and the messages through her words and her body language.

Closure: Have her pick one final card from the unread cards. This card is a final thought for her reading. It might act as a kind of summary card.

2. A Tarot Reading with a Hint of the Sight

Grounding: Lay out a few decks. Let the seeker select the one she resonates with creatively. Put the desired deck face down between you. Invite the seeker to put her fingertips on the edge of the deck as you do the same. Suggest she breathe deeply as she senses the center of her being, wherever that might be today. The suggestion might be, "See yourself falling to your center easily like a feather, swaying from side to side as you float down."

Intent: Ask her to shuffle or mix the order of the cards as she lets go of the world. Inform her that you will be grounding a little deeper. Gently close your eyes. Silently ask her higher self and/or Divine committee to send a genuine story of her spirit. What is needed for this session, for her path?

Share this image with her. Explore her intentions for this reading. If there are no clear ones, you might ask, "If you had a magic wand and you could change anything in your life, what would you change?" This question is always a good place to start.

Form: The first spread serves well as an overview of her life currently. Any spread will do as long as its design can show various facets of her life. Two or three major themes or areas needing fresh insight will often surface during this overview spread. Suggest those themes as options for exploration. The seeker may have a number of questions as well. It may not be possible or prudent to fit them all in. Assure her that the relevant questions will be answered one way or another.

Let's use the Wellsian Celtic Spread (chapter 14) as the overview spread for a well-rounded, big-picture view of her life and reality. Have her pick two cards face down that will represent her current core rhythms. You will lay out the rest of the cards face down in the Wellsian spread.

During the rest of the reading, use Path Spreads (chapter 14). This simple format of a line of cards captures the stories and influences needed. Simply lay down three to six cards for each of her specific questions and issues.

Synchronicity: What of the initial image? Treat it as if it were the corner piece of a jigsaw puzzle. Does any other information from the seeker, the cards, or her Divine committee connect with the initial image? Continue fitting the pieces into the puzzle as you read the rest of the cards in the spread and receive new psychic clues.

During the overview spread, invite her to focus on one of the core cards. Ask questions about her sense of these cards such as, "If the card represents a snapshot of your life right now, what would that mean to you? How would you say this story is manifesting itself in your life? How would you describe the energy or essence of this card? What does it trigger for you?"

Listen to the way she responds to both of these major theme cards. Without judgment, hear her observations about her life. Also listen to what is not being said—do you sense feelings or energy behind her words?

Let the cards speak to you. Some will be loud and others will only whisper. Not all cards carry equal importance. Focus on the ones that speak to the heart of the matter. The images will reveal to you what you need to know. Trust what you really see. Speak with compassion about these messages.

Closure: This act of intimate exploration needs a closing ritual. Have the seeker choose one card from the unused part of the deck. Suggest aloud that this card's image will offer a last insight before she returns to the world of daily rhythms and responsibilities.

Integration: After reading this last card, suggest she not think of the specifics of the reading for the next forty-eight hours. Encourage her to use this time to allow her deeper wisdom to surface. Have her pay attention to dreams and synchronicity. Hopefully, the reading will be a catalyst for her own wisdom.

If your preferred style of reading uses the tarot as the main messenger, embrace extensive tarot study. Exposure to the traditional definitions and spreads, as well as other systems such as numerology, astrology, symbolism (especially Hebrew, Christian, and Kabala), and archetypes, would contribute greatly to your effectiveness. Over time, this body of knowledge will become layers of definitions for each card.

3. A Tarot and Psychic Reading

In this variation of reading, the reader is an active consultant working in partnership with the seeker's higher self, guides, ancestors and even the seeker's psyche selves. New insights and support of the seeker's current needs are revealed through this team effort.

Grounding: Tell the seeker to close her eyes and think of little else besides breathing slowly and fully. After a minute or two, give her an exercise to focus her energy, such as bringing in all of her "octopus arms" from the world. She should feel the totality of her focus and energy. She needs to let everyone and everything else wait outside the door for her.

Intent: Have her swirl the cards face down in a big messy pile, thinking of all the potential available for her life as you continue to meditate. Silently request an initial image. Speak to her of the initial image. Does it trigger her thoughts in any way? After gathering her expectations and the story of the initial image, discuss an intent for the reading that she agrees with heartily.

Form: Either have her gather all the cards together into one group or have her select from the messy pile throughout the reading. The Circle Spread (chapter 14) will act as the overview reading. Have her select one card face down. This card represents the beginning for the session and is placed as the center card. Lay three to six cards around the center. They will represent the topics that need introspection, exploration, or attention.

Synchronicity: Does the Circle Spread continue the ideas raised by her questions and the initial image? What does this overview reading suggest in terms of the direction of the reading?

During the entire process, listen carefully to any loving voice that speaks on her behalf. The Divine beings of this group might include her ancestors who have influenced the behaviors and deep beliefs of her bloodline, departed loved ones, and her psyche selves. The cards will bring the imagery needed to mirror these messages and messengers.

It is imperative to listen unconditionally. At times, the questions that arise are more fruitful than the answers received. If the seeker should feel this flow of information to be too much like therapy, bring the message back to the tangible benefits in her life. For example, if she would like to be in a relationship and isn't finding anyone remotely interesting, ask her Lover psyche to show up and give you the inside scoop. Ask questions of the Lover psyche such as, "Do you want to be in a relationship? What are the pros and cons of sharing life with another? What do you mistrust when you open up your heart and underbelly? What do you gain?" Ask questions while choosing a few cards as responses from the Lover psyche. This dialogue can yield powerful new perspectives and solutions.

Closure: Gather all the cards. Select one card as a blessing of any of the insights that are ready and willing to surface.

Integration: Suggest the seeker spend a few hours creating a vision board about ideas from the session that triggered excitement or passion. The vision board is a collage of images selected from magazines. These pictures are selected quickly, as they catch the eye and heart, without the processing and categorization of the logical mind. The board is made within a time limit, usually around an hour. The board aids its maker in connecting to the ideas that offer nourishment in life.

4. A Psychic Reading with a Hint of Tarot

In this type of reading, the Sight is the compass pointing north. Tarot cards act as guideposts, picked sparingly to clarify statements, affirm direction, or respond to questions during the session.

Grounding: Have several tarot decks lined up for the seeker. Have her pick the one deck with which she resonates artistically. Hold the deck as you say aloud, "We ask for the Creative Unknown to bring us clarity, guidance, and peace."

Intent: Have her mix the deck in any way she chooses. Say, "Let the cards absorb all the pros and cons of your life as if they were cosmic sponges. Pick one card whenever you feel finished." Inform her you will ground deeper as you close your eyes and ask for the initial image in silence.

Form: Over the course of the entire reading, you may lay only one or two cards per issue. You are listening and gathering information. You would draw to reflect the seeker's current challenges and choices.

Synchronicity: Imagine all the seeker's questions and concerns, as well as the initial image, entering a timeless labyrinth. The twists and turns of this exploration are leading to the center, the essence of loving her life. Listen well to her questions and responses as you receive guidance from any Divine overseers, departed loved ones, ancestors, and those parts of her unconscious representing aspects of her personality. Pull cards whenever clarification is needed.

With the past, present, and future time all together, you and the seeker become time travelers. Not only do you listen to the psyche selves, you witness the actual environment alongside the seeker. You are the invisible companion and witness to the internal movies and messages that keep replaying. You will view relevant scenarios that create fear or love in her life.

This journey requires you to go deeper and further than as a witness and negotiator. As an observer of the seeker's internal landscapes, you can shine the light and name the things that the seeker cannot or has not claimed for himself.

Since the third style is very experiential, you need to be well-grounded with a strong sense of self, humor, and spirit. It is an honor to have this kind of access. Encourage the seeker to see herself as the hero of her story. That alone brings a power she may not be trusting. The seeker is no longer alone in her narrative. By your presence, she also becomes the present-day leader with open eyes and ears to those old needs. The light, the dark, and the shadows of her life are no longer censored or ignored.

This style raises the opportunity for creative questions such as:

- What is the best and the worst that could happen?
- What would it feel like if she did this differently?
- How could this change her everyday life?
- What part of her life is still a reenactment of an outdated belief?
- What needs to shift?

Closure: Have her pick one last card as the secret of the reading. What one last idea needs to sneak in?

Integration: Sum up the various action steps or new ideas that you encountered during this reading. Have her play with the pertinent ideas in some tangible, creative way over the next forty-eight hours.

5. A Psychic Reading

This reading is much like the former style, but there are no visual aids at all. You are not only the witness to her inner life, but will at times speak up as her negotiator through a creative dialogue with her fears, hidden desires, and unconscious reactions and training. It is essential that you move gracefully, with curiosity and respect. Your role as witness now has the added quality of questioning authority, such as old beliefs. The psyche selves are often helpful in revealing where there may be stagnation or un- met needs.

Grounding: Breathe deeply as you silently ask for an ini- tial image of her current relationship to this life. Have the seeker speak her full name three times aloud. Listen carefully to all your senses. What do you hear behind her voice? What guides are nearby? Are there certain parts of her that are making themselves known already?

Intent: After talking to her about ideas and images you may have received, explore the questions and areas she would like to discuss. Do not push any connections, but simply let the different impressions from her and her Di- vine committee flow uninterrupted.

Form: Scribbling or holding a crystal might be some ways of giving yourself permission to receive the sideways information from her Divine committee. Closing your eyes and taking rich pauses are necessary to ground and integrate the flow of information. Without the imagery of the cards, your mind will now provide the relevant stories. This often feels like an internal movie or short story.

Synchronicity: Encourage her to share her thoughts and feelings from the stories and messages you receive. In this dialogue, you will get a real sense of the current state of love within her life: Is she tolerating it, or is it a burden? Does she feel like she would love to change her life but has little hope or energy to do so? What exactly would she love to change? What does that change look like in everyday life? Rather than give ready-made solutions, ask questions about the validity and effectiveness of her present choices and perspectives. Witness her life with the full light of her spirit all around the both of you. Speak of the ways you sense her energies without judgment or apology. Name her psyche selves in terms of their archetypes, such as the Little One or the Worker. Give voice to those parts of herself that show themselves to you. Providing a sacred space with respect and truth will undoubtedly bring fresh new insights.

Closure: Invite her to select three words that best capture the essence of this session. Have her close her eyes as you softly repeat the three words aloud.

Integration: Speak of one image or message that seems to bring hope and passion. Suggest creative ways she can bring that message to life by surrounding herself with a particular image or words.

Final Thoughts

Tarot with Sight is potent in any proportion. The six principles will always serve you well. Don't underestimate the strength and love that surround you once you call for Sight during the Grounding. Let the beauty of this short life come pouring in before choosing a true direction during the intent. Let new patterns arise in the solid structures of form. Use the magic of synchronicity. Consult, negotiate, and advocate for the seeker's love of life. Find this magic in everyday life during integration.

19

Helpful Boundaries

The Devil is in the details

Tarot within the Sight is a strong, valuable tool in navigating realities and with this power comes the responsibility of boundaries, not only with information you receive for others, but for yourself as well. As you learn and grow as a reader, you may branch out into unfamiliar territory in your relationships with others and the Divine. What lines must be drawn in relation to cosmic information? You'll find that like most things, it depends on the situation.

Boundaries with Strangers

When you mindfully read energy in the world, are there times when you should let others know the information received? Say you tune in to your intuitive awareness for practice at a restaurant. You realize a young man two tables away has recently lost a loved one and is considering abusing alcohol to cope. Do you go try to talk him out of it?

The answer is an emphatic "no." It is not a good idea to volunteer information to people who have not asked for a reading. Just because you receive information does not mean a person is ready to hear it. When people are ready, they will seek you out.

I HAVE SET MY OWN PERSONAL BOUNDARY TO ONLY READ FOR THOSE WHO ASK FOR A READING.

Boundaries with Family and Friends

Most readers don't use their skills for family, much like doctors or therapists not using their professional skills for their families: it's difficult to be an impartial witness with family members. The temptation might be to censor difficult information, judge decision making, or fail to listen to them with the respectful mystery that comes easily with a stranger. On their part, your family may not listen to the wisdom flowing through you either. To read for family requires a very strong and open relationship of trust, wherein you and your family member are on equal footing, at least for the session's duration. It also requires you to be absolutely impartial, even and especially with difficult information. You and your family are generally so intertwined on an energetic level that this goal is incredibly challenging. As boundaries go, not reading for family is a good one to have.

Reading for friends can be a different proposition. As with strangers, you don't want to impose a reading or information received from one of your own readings. You may be quite excited about your newfound tarot skills, but it is better to be asked for a reading.

Another challenging aspect of reading for friends or family is that these are people you will see again and again. A difficult reading can cause friction for years. But even that is not as difficult as having one of your readings misrepresented over and over. If you end up discussing the readings again later (and inevitably you will), you may find the relative/significant other/friend didn't hear the intended message. You need to allow for different interpretations and selective memories. You need to release the reading—the wisdom that comes from it is up to the seeker alone.

Boundaries with Seekers/Clients

Whether they are strangers or friends, anyone who comes to you for a reading should be able to expect certain things from you, and you from them. A necessary boundary is confidentiality. What is spoken between the reader and the seeker stays at the table. Consider the idea of sacred amnesia, a letting go of the reading during closure so that no memory of it can surface for anyone but the seeker. If for some reason the reader has information concerning others from a self-reading, the privacy then belongs between the reader and the Creative Unknown. The reader does not volunteer this information to anyone unless there is implied harm such as child or elder abuse, suicide, or homicide.

The reader is not responsible for what the seeker does with the information gleaned from a reading. A reading is to be given openly and mindfully, and is a sacred exchange. The responsibility ends when the reading ends.

I read for a co-worker back in my waitressing days. Over the days following the reading, I was shocked to discover she was having a breakdown. She was incoherent, irrational, and seemingly unaware of concrete reality, yet quoting lucidly word for word the messages received during the reading.

A couple of friends and I took her to the hospital, fearing for her safety. I talked to the doctor after they admitted her to the psych ward. I told him I felt awful that my reading had put her over the edge. The doctor told me it was not my fault. She was having a full-blown episode of a mental disorder (the name of which I can't recall) and would have latched on to any excuse to check out. In this case, it happened to be my tarot reading. I realized I can't be responsible for what somebody does with a tarot reading. I can only be responsible for it being given with as much love and clarity as possible.

A reader *is* responsible for the emotional safety and spiritual comfort of the seeker during the reading. Leave your projections and judgments at the door. The seeker needs to be comfortable sharing with you, and you need to be respectful of his or her life path.

If you have managed to create a space where a seeker can let go, tears and raw emotions are inevitable. Acknowledge and honor the seeker's reactions. Tears are a natural release. Hostility is a natural defense. Fear produces all kinds of emotional states. To move through emotional reactions with grace and ease to get to the heart of the matter, take nothing personally.

Relay difficult information with sensitivity and kindness. At the same time, don't sanitize the juice out of the insight. Present it cleanly and simply without apology. If you are treating the seeker with kid gloves, you are most likely underestimating his or her ability to handle difficult information.

Offer good resources such as specific books, organizations, or practitioners that can serve the seeker well. Any medical or legal information needs to be checked with professionals trained in those fields. Encourage them to make decisions from a well-informed and loving place. The reading serves as just one of those sources.

Be respectful of time, yours and theirs. Try not to run over your designated time with the seeker. Once the insight starts flowing, it sometimes seems like the reading could go on forever. Honor both of you by keeping the reading to the agreed time. Also, whether it is your work or hobby, designate times to read for others rather than being "on call." This small rule creates a structure that may actually aid in building your energetic muscles.

Allow time between readings. A reading will usually uncover one or several aspects of the seeker's life that need to be absorbed and integrated. The seeker should take the time to do some of this work before returning for more.

I SUGGEST TO MY CLIENTS THAT THE NEXT FULL READING BE THREE TO SIX MONTHS FROM OUR LAST READING, UNLESS WE ENTER A COACHING RELATIONSHIP.

Often you and the seeker will unearth areas that need a great deal of work. Throughout any divination, the reader may detect troubling patterns, such as chronic depression. In some instances, there may appear a flirtation with suicide, spoken or unspoken. Whether it be a medical, emotional, or physical imbalance, readers need to be clear about their expertise to sense the unknown. The seeker needs to be encouraged to find professional support and to never substitute his or her judgment for another's.

As I was reading for a client, I received an image of her fantasizing about suicide, though she didn't appear outwardly depressed. I received images of brief scenarios that seemed to flicker across her mind just

before bed or in the shower. At that point I said, "I'm
wondering if, and you don't need to answer this if it
doesn't make you feel comfortable, but I'm wondering
if every once in a great while you fantasize with the
idea of leaving this life because it's so hard?" The client
was both bewildered and bemused by my knowing
this. She nodded her head yes.

I said, "You know, the only real control we have in
this life is ending it. Could we make suicide option Z
and use this reading to see options of A through Y?"

To her credit, she listened as best she could. The
areas causing great pressure and stress were revealed.
She accepted the major suggestions to seek professional
therapy, drink a lot of water, and sleep eight hours
nightly as much as possible.

Suicidal thoughts are toxic and should never be treated
casually. A long-term relationship with a therapist would
be far more beneficial than a one-hour reading, no matter
how insightful.

Boundaries with the Divine

All relationships have an inherent contract of agreements,
and it's no different with the Divine. A contract for a mu-
tually respectful relationship requires awareness and clear
communication. It's recommended you compose a physical contract for the work you'll do with the Divine.

List at least five things you need to feel both mentally and emotionally secure as you prepare to embark on the next phase of your psychic journey. This is your opportunity to tell the universe what you need from it to go forward. Do you need an ironclad guarantee that you aren't going to go off the deep end? Write it down. Do you feel a need for strong direction and guidance from the Creative Unknown? Write it down.

When you are satisfied with your list, do something to seal the deal. Sign a printed document. Paint it. Sew it. Draw it. Sculpt it. Build a mosaic on your wall. Do whatever feels right to seal this pact between you and the Universe. Keep it some place you can see it and refer back to it. Sometimes you just need to know there's a net to catch you as you fly towards the next trapeze bar. Here's an example of a completed contract:

Contract with My Guides

Herein I will detail what I need from my guides that I might go forward to complete my lifespan on this path, which they have stressed is so important I complete.

1. To proceed, I cannot go back into the dark again. I fear I will not have the strength to return a second time. I need the help and resources necessary not to descend that far again in this life cycle. If it was preordained that I need to spend more time there, then I ask for it to be spread out more over successive lives, because this one has become quite fragile,

and I fear I will not complete this life's mission if I have to go back there again.

2. I need more direction. I desire not just to be punished or rewarded for being on or off the path and left in limbo about whether I am on or off until I am punished. Life on this plane is uncertain enough. Give me guidance. At least then if I run into a tree, I'll know it was my own fault for not listening.

   a. If this is a situation where you are telling me and I'm just not getting the message, teach me how to hear you, please.

   b. If this is a situation where you believe I will find the right way on my own, no matter how many trees I run into, I thank you for your faith in me, but please, to quote Mother Teresa, don't "trust me so much."

3. I thank you for keeping me physically safe. My faith in your abilities to keep me mentally and emotionally safe has been severely damaged, however. Please be patient with me and help me learn trust.

4. Please help me have a fuller understanding of my relationship to you and better communication with you.

5. Help me be a light in the dark.

Boundaries with Yourself

It is possible, with practice, to set boundaries on when you receive insights. Set an intention to receive information during certain times, and only when grounded, unless it is a dire warning. A reader is not a 24/7 seer, nor should one aspire to be. It is not wise, or even safe. Know, and make sure the universe also knows, when your spiritual shingle is out and when it is not.

It is terribly tempting to feel responsible for the information you pass on to seekers, but know you are not. Make a practice to not isolate, fix, or carry any energies besides your own during or after a session. Readers are not merging or losing themselves in any sense of the word. Actually, the opposite is true—readers should be well grounded in their own being. Remember this idea; it will serve you for all of your life!

Refrain from reading under the influence of drugs or alcohol. It would even be a good plan to cut out caffeine (yes, even tea) and nicotine before a reading. Drink water before, during, and after instead. It helps keep you grounded and alert.

Take a break from reading if you're experiencing loopy or obsessive thinking, or if you begin to entertain such feelings as paranoia or nervousness. Asking the same question in different ways or reading because you crave approval are also unhealthy patterns. These are all signs to put this work down for a while for necessary integration.

And lastly, dance that tango well with your own ego. Your ego can't be attached to the readings you give. People will take what they want and leave the rest … and so should you.

20

※

TRAITS OF A TRUE READER

Sound strategy comes from fearless love

Remember the earlier metaphor of intuition as a piano? Each one of us came with one into this life. The way we use it makes the difference. Continuing the same analogy, it's possible to list attributes of a good pianist, such as having a good sense of rhythm, pitch, discipline, and even the need to sound out melodies. But there are plenty of talented pianists who won't fit into broad categories such as these. It's possible to be a brilliant pianist with short fingers or little training. Keep in mind that as you read this chapter, you may be unacknowledged and still a true reader in every sense.

As a child, the potential reader may have received labels such as "big mouth" or "too curious for your own good." Chances are, this child enjoyed invisible beings, picture books, and mythological figures a lot earlier and for much longer than other children. From a very young age, things were not always what they appeared to be. During adolescence or as a young adult, a person like this may have served as a confidant to many. Even strangers could be drawn to this person's way of listening and non-judgmental patience.

Readers tend to be strong communicators. They have a love of translating energy, imagery, lofty ideas, and emotions into proactive ideas, knowledge, and wisdom. They listen well, with their eyes and hearts as well as with their ears. These empathetic skills serve the rest of us well in terms of dealing with the ambiguity of simply being a human.

Those with the Sight have a love affair with life. They connect to a greater source of love or greatly sense the separateness. Transformation trumps comfort. The forces of nature, art, philosophy, and love are sources for the integration of the body, mind, and spirit. Readers of energy luxuriate in mystery, loving its twists and turns. Paradoxes and metaphors are fun sandboxes to play in, humor a familiar lifeline.

These lifelong learners are passionate about creativity, psychology, anthropology, and/or storytelling. A dedicated practitioner is continually updating his or her studies and connecting with peers to become more resourceful for clients.

Somebody who is deeply committed to this kind of work pushes the edge of his or her own creative growth. These people tend to have good detective skills, such as gathering clues and patiently waiting for bigger pictures and clearer messages to appear.

This seer would not confuse the message with the messenger, even when others do. Whether such an accusation is false flattery or angry resentment, there is a clear sense of self and service. There is no messianic confusion, even though it may have felt like a calling since childhood.

A true reader is really a teacher. A teacher helps others wake up to their own Creative Authority.

APPENDIX A

THE SEVENTY-EIGHT TAROT CARDS

Every picture tells a story

Within these next pages appear all seventy-eight cards of a traditional deck—Lo Scarabeo's Universal Tarot by Roberto de Angelis, to be exact. The cards are separated by arcana and suit: swords, wands, cups, and pentacles. They appear in their numeric order. A new deck will be ordered in much the same way. These images will serve as good guides to spark your intuition, clarify certain visual parts of the text, or at least start a familiarization with tarot and its imagery until the time comes for you to find your own deck.

APPENDIX B

❧

SELF-STUDY GUIDE

In time, all integration happens

To become a great reader, it's important to practice! This guide includes all the exercises throughout the book with a few variations and some additional suggestions, as well as corresponding chapters in this book. After reading it over, commit to completing the exercises within a certain timeline, such as a season or a year and a day. Your timeline will apply to some of the exercises, especially the first three. Intent makes for receptivity! Explore and enjoy.

- ❑ Put away all tarot reference and definitions books. Commit to strengthening your own Creative Authority through only listening to your perceptions for at least one season. ("Before You Begin")

- ❑ Prepare a study journal by devoting a few pages for each of the seventy-eight cards, a whole section for the three families (court cards, the four suits and the major arcana), and another full section for synchronicity. Note significant insights gained from a card, an exercise, or a spread. Record initial thoughts or any intuitive ideas stirred by reading the book. ("Before You Begin")

❑ Choose one deck that will serve as your learning tool. ("Before You Begin")

❑ Write about current ideas and attitudes about psychic and tarot abilities. What is a concern about becoming very accomplished at both? Is this answer in any way tied to older training? What would be a vision of yourself if your psychic and tarot abilities were fluent? (Chapter 1)

❑ If your cards are new, remove the outer casing and house the cards in a favorite scarf, bag, or box. If your cards are used, bless them with a smudge stick or some other purifying instrument. (Chapter 3)

❑ Envision being given the four sacred tools of your soul: the sword, the wand, the cup, and the pentacle. What would each one feel like? Look like? If the sword cuts through falsehoods, the wand creates magic, the cup contains the flow of your emotions, and the pentacle is a protective healing object, which do you most need now? (Chapter 4)

❑ Dedicate a week to each of the four suits. Try to find them in the natural world. Concentrate on each of their specific gifts and challenges in your life. (Chapter 4)

❑ *Light and Shadow.* Pick two cards from each suit. One card is your natural strength, the other a shadow card reflecting a weak point. Interpret these cards, keeping in mind the essence of each suit. (Chapter 4)

❑ Write a short story about the kind of royalty found in each of the elemental kingdoms. (Chapter 5)

❑ Lay out all of your court cards. Match each card to the people you have come to know in this lifetime— good, bad, and indifferent. In particular, find your mother, father, and yourself. (Chapter 5)

❑ Look at each court card for a component of your personality and nature. Give them archetypal titles such as daughter, wife, worker, dreamer, procrastinator, etc. (Chapter 5)

❑ Write a description of each court card as pure energy. (Chapter 5)

❑ *Good Cop, Bad Cop.* Look through all of your major arcana cards. Pick your favorite and least favorite. Study the beloved in terms of the things that you are learning and loving well at this time. Look at the disliked one in light of resistances and fears. (Chapter 6)

❑ As you look at the favored major arcana from the preceding exercise, ask yourself, what would be the pitfalls? Now look at the disliked one and ask yourself, what could I really gain from this energy? (Chapter 6)

❑ *Turning Point One.* Record fifteen turning points that have made you who you are today. Find major arcana cards that most capture each of these experience. Repeat cards are possible. (Chapter 6)

❑ Jot down the first thing that comes to your mind while answering the Chapter 6 version of *The Fool's Journey.* What insights are received when reading those answers in light of the corresponding major arcana? (Chapter 6)

0. I wish I was heading towards _____

1. I am becoming _____

2. I secretly know that _____

3. I desire _____

4. I am thinking pretty clearly about _____

5. I believe in _____

6. I am in love with _____

7. I am driven by _____

8. My biggest challenge these days is _____

9. My inner voice tells me to _____

10. Lately, I describe the circumstances in my life as _____

11. Truthfully, I would like to say that _____

12. I see my life very differently since _____

13. I am done with _____

14. I am being guided to _____

15. My greatest fear is becoming _____

16. I seriously need to change _____

17. I accept _____

18. A dream holding my deepest desires is _____

19. I am open to _____

20. I am reawakening to _____

21. My destiny is _____

Now lay out your major arcana and compare each answer to its corresponding major arcana by number. Keep in mind that this exercise was designed with the most common chronology of the major arcana order: 0 Fool, 1 The Magician, 2 The High Priestess, 3 The Empress, 4 The Emperor, 5 The Hierophant, 6 The Lovers, 7 The Chariot, 8 Strength, 9 The Hermit, 10 The Wheel of Fortune, 11 Justice, 12 The Hanged Man, 13 Death, 14 Temperance, 15 The Devil, 16 The Tower, 17 The Star, 18 The Moon, 19 The Sun, 20 Judgement, and 21 The World. (Chapter 6)

❑ *Turning Point Two.* Think of one major event that changed the direction of your life that might need resolution, clarity, or new insight. Shuffle only the major arcana as you focus on the aspects of that event. Pick one card and hold it near you without looking at the face. Are there any shifts or new ideas? Look at the card. Does it have more to say? (Chapter 6)

❑ Receive impressions by closing your eyes and listening. (Chapter 7)

❑ While waiting in a store line, try to see everyone in the line next to you as they may have appeared in their favorite past life. (Chapter 7)

❑ *Mystery Images.* Cut ten images from old magazines. Put each one in indistinguishable envelopes. Hold each envelope and write any triggers on the envelope itself. Rate each trigger on a scale of 1 to 10, 10 being a hit, 1 being a wild guess, 5 signifying uncertainty. Open each envelope. Is there any connection or relevance between the energy you read and the image? (Chapter 7)

❑ *Dead or Alive.* Ask a friend to focus on someone she loves well, living or passed. Focus silently on the person she's thinking of. Without help, answer if the person is dead or alive, female or male, and light or dark skinned; ask their age their body build and the message they have for your partner. (Chapter 7)

❑ Start noticing the daily workings of intuition and synchronicity. Record at least three events daily. For example: Which elevator door did you think would open? How many bills are waiting in your mail? Who called just when you were thinking of them? (Chapter 7)

❑ Record your current beliefs about the Divine, ghosts, spirits, and other invisible beings. What was one of your favorite experiences? Where have your beliefs veered from your training? What would you like to believe? (Chapter 8)

❏ Starting with your mother and father, visualize walking past each ancestor to get to the one who has a freedom or gift for you. (Chapter 8)

❏ Write about past lives that you might have had. What is your favorite music? Fashion? Literature? Explore all of your innate tastes and preference, and create a story of the past life that has most influenced this one. What do you think is the karma? What is a repeating theme for you in this life? (Chapter 8)

❏ Touch base with a loved one who has passed. Speak out loud to him or her and have a conversation. Listen as well. (Chapter 8)

❏ Either through writing or meditation, discover your Divine committee. If you could meet the six to ten guides or teachers from the other side who are your Divine support, who would they be? Who do you think is helping you grow already? Who would you prefer to see on your committee? (Chapter 8)

❏ *Bathtub Meditation.* Run a bath for yourself. Focus on one destructive or distracting behavior you have had for a long time. Visualize all the women in your bloodline starting with your mother, her mother, and her mother all the way back to the beginning of your gene pool. Walk past each one until you sense the one woman who is the source of your current fear or dysfunction. If you can see her face, ask her to tell you her story. Why did this start? What were her choices? Tell her how the issue has manifested in your life. Ask her to help release you from this grip. You can also perform this envisioning your father and male family members as well. (Chapter 8)

❑ Explore a friend's psyche selves, particularly those who may be raising a ruckus or causing a stalemate in your friend's life. (Chapter 9)

❑ *The Destiny Self.* Ask your future self who has completely manifested his or her destiny what he or she thinks of your current path. For fifteen minutes, just color or scribble. Stay receptive to new ideas or a message. (Chapter 10)

❑ *The Hidden Questions.* Write three pertinent questions in your life on separate sheets of paper. Seal each into indistinguishable envelopes. Every day for a week after a five-minute minute meditation, record any trigger or idea received while holding each envelope. After a week, open each envelope. What messages did you receive? Any surprises? How do you connect the answers to the question? (Chapter 10)

❑ *The Sideways Exercise.* Record a question or request. Take the next half hour to pay attention to all the events happening in the environment. Write anything that grabbed your focus in the order it happened. After the time is up, write your associations for each event you recorded. See if a story surfaces when you read the associations out loud. (Chapter 10)

❑ *The Initial Image.* Ask a friend to focus on an issue or area that could use some different insight. Close your eyes. Ask for a story or movie of her current state of being. Keep this in mind. Have her form a question concerning the issue. How does the initial movie or message speak to this question? For about ten minutes, tell her any images or messages you receive, starting with the first one. After that time, have her tell you what resonated with her. (Chapter 11)

❑ Experiment with different forms of grounding. What does it take to turn down the chatter in your mind? Research some breathing techniques easily found in yoga literature. (Chapter 12)

❑ Hold your cards as you think of a pressing question. As you shuffle or mix the cards, let the question expand in your mind and heart. What is the true question behind it? What is its deepest mystery? (Chapter 13)

❑ Shuffle so some of the cards will be reversed as you concentrate on a single intent. Pick cards until you receive one reversed card. If this image was a subtle message of hidden perspectives of this intent, what would those be? What was your first visual cue with it upside down? (Chapter 14)

❑ *One Card.* Pick one card every morning for at least a month for the way you will best serve the day in love. A true understanding of this card will be revealed to you before bedtime. (Chapter 14)

❑ Pick a card every evening before bedtime. This card is the Divine's Kodak moment of your day. Do you recognize those energies? Do you agree? (Chapter 14)

❑ *Three-Card Spread of Position.* Designate three different positions for each card, such as past, present, and future. Read the cards in the designated context. (Chapter 14)

❑ *Three-Card in Layers.* Read three chosen cards literally, symbolically, and psychically. How do the three layers change or deepen the story? (Chapter 14)

❑ *A Path Spread.* Read three to seven cards in a story form. Start with the exposition, go to the climax, and finish with the resolution. You may explore one path or several paths, depending on the issue. How does the resulting story reflect your question or intent? (Chapter 14)

❑ *A Circle Spread.* Focus on one intent or area. Choose one card to designate you in the center with three to six cards circling the center all face down. Turn each card over and interpret it in relation to you as the center. (Chapter 14)

❑ *A Traditional Celtic Cross Spread.* Use this classic format for a detailed response to a question or intent that needs clarification. (Chapter 14)

❑ *A Wellsian Celtic Cross Variation Spread.* As you shuffle the cards, see your current life as a movie.

What has been on your radar lately? What are the strongest themes running through your life? Use the Wellsian Celtic Cross format to gain fresh insights. (Chapter 14)

❑ *An Essence Spread.* Separate the cards into the four suits, the court cards, and the major arcana. Gain a valuable inventory of your current energies through the Essence Spread. (Chapters 4, 5, 6)

❑ Look through the deck for the card you would truly like to experience. Place it under your pillow. Before falling asleep, say aloud that you will remember the dream given in response. (Chapter 8)

❑ Commit to one action step from each reading for yourself. (Chapter 17)

❑ Read for another person using the tarot as the primary information source. (Chapter 18)

❑ Read for another person using the tarot as well as insights from the initial image. (Chapter 18)

❑ Read for another person using the tarot cards only as road posts during the session. (Chapter 18)

❑ *Divine Contract.* Create a written contract listing the support and requirements you will need with your Divine team as you open to your intuition. (Chapter 19)

❑ Envision a day in your life with you in your full Creative Authority. How would it feel different? The same?

*We hope this book has triggered deeper wisdom,
common sense, and creative freedom for you.
The six principles will be a sturdy net.
Keep learning and growing.
Trust your own pace and rhythms.*

*Stories tell us who we are.
Readings help us change the stories.*

BIBLIOGRAPHY

Books to stir your Creative Authority

Bodine, Echo L. *A Still, Small Voice: A Psychic's Guide to Awakening Intuition*. Novato, CA: New World Library, 2001.

Cameron, Julia. *The Artist's Way: A Spiritual Path to Higher Creativity*. New York: J.P. Tarcher/Putnam, 2002.

Choquette, Sonia. *Ask Your Guides: Connecting to Your Divine Support System*. Carlsbad, CA: Hay House, 2006.

———. *Diary of a Psychic: Shattering the Myths*. Carlsbad, CA: Hay House, 2003.

———. *The Psychic Pathway: A Workbook for Reawakening the Voice of Your Soul*. New York: Carol Trade Paperbacks, 1995.

Dickerman, Alexandra Collins. *Following Your Path: Using Myths, Symbols, and Images to Explore Your Inner Life*. Los Angeles: J.P. Tarcher, 1992.

Edwards, Betty. *The New Drawing on the Right Side of the Brain*. London: HarperCollins, 2008.

Fairfield, Gail. *Choice Centered Tarot*. York Beach, ME: Samuel Weiser, 1997.

Greer, Mary K. *21 Ways to Read a Tarot Card*. Woodbury, MN: Llewellyn Publications, 2008.

Jayanti, Amber. *Living the Tarot: Applying an Ancient Oracle to the Challenges of Modern Life*. St. Paul, MN: Llewellyn Publications, 1993.

Kenner, Corrine. *Simple Fortunetelling with Tarot Cards: Corrine Kenner's Complete Guide*. Woodbury, MN: Llewellyn Publications, 2007.

———. *Tarot for Writers*. Woodbury, MN: Llewellyn Publications, 2009.

Livon, Jodi. *The Happy Medium: Awakening to Your Natural Intuition*. Woodbury, MN: Llewellyn Publications, 2009.

Nichols, Sallie. *Jung and Tarot: An Archetypal Journey*. York Beach, ME: Samuel Weiser, 1988.

Pollack, Rachel. *Seventy-Eight Degrees of Wisdom: A Book of Tarot*. London: Thorsons, 1997.

———. *Tarot Wisdom: Spiritual Teachings and Deeper Meanings*. Woodbury, MN: Llewellyn Publications, 2008.